Mattie,

May God

grace a. peace

In your storms

of Life

R. Lobil

Hebrews 12:1-2

Weathering
the Storms *of* Life

Ricky D. Bishop

CROSSBOOKS·
PUBLISHING

CrossBooks™
A Division of LifeWay
1663 Liberty Drive
Bloomington, IN 47403
www.crossbooks.com
Phone: 1-866-879-0502

First published by CrossBooks: 09/18/2012

ISBN: 978-1-4627-2141-2 (sc)
ISBN: 978-1-4627-2142-9 (e)
ISBN: 978-1-4627-2143-6 (hc)

Library of Congress Control Number: 2012916796

Printed in the United States of America

This book is printed on acid-free paper.

The Rainy Day

The day is cold, and dark, and dreary;
It rains, and the wind is never weary;
The vine still clings to the moldering wall,
But at every gust the dead leaves fall,
And the day is dark and dreary.

My life is cold, and dark, and dreary;
It rains, and the wind is never weary;
My thoughts still cling to the moldering Past,
But the hopes of youth fall thick in the blast
And the days are dark and dreary.

Be still, sad heart! and cease repining;
Behind the clouds is the sun still shining;
Thy fate is the common fate of all,
Into each life some rain must fall,
Some days must be dark and dreary.

Henry Wadsworth Longfellow

CONTENTS

Section I.   Preparing for the Storm –
(Mark 4:35-41) / ix
Storm Preparation / x

Chapter 1. The Unique Opportunity for Fellowship / 1

Chapter 2. The Unexpected Occasion of a Storm / 5

Chapter 3. The Unquestionable Object of Faith / 11

Section II.   Finding Peace in the Storm
– (Mark 6:45-52) / 16
Tracking the Storm / 17

Chapter 1. Often God's Purposes are Hard to
Understand in the Storm / 19

Chapter 2. Often God's Timing is Hard to Understand / 25

Chapter 3. Often God's Answers are Hard to Understand / 29

Chapter 4. Often We Never Understand but We Grow / 35

Chapter 5. The Ultimate Result of the Storm / 40

Section III.   Finding Power to Overcome the
Storm – (Matthew 14:27-33) / 46
Playing in the Storm / 47

Chapter 1. Peter's Radical Request / 49

Chapter 2. Peters Risky Walk / 53

Chapter 3. The Progressive Growth / 57

**Section IV.   Finding our Priorities in the
            Storm – (Acts 27:1-44) / 63**
The Loss to the Storm / 67

Chapter 1. The Danger of Calm Seas / 70

Chapter 2. Losing Control to the Storm / 75

Chapter 3. Losing Dreams in the Storm / 78

Chapter 4. Finding Hope in the Storm / 82

**Section V.   Facing Personal Responsibility
            in the Storm – (Jonah) / 87**
Responsibility / 90

Chapter 1. The Disobedient Prophet / 91

Chapter 2. The Providence of God / 95

Chapter 3. The Fish Belly Prayers / 99

Chapter 4. The Fish Puke Prophet / 105

**Section VI.   Recovering from the Storm
            – Genesis 9 / 110**
Storm Recovery / 113

Chapter 1. The Ultimate Storm / 115

Chapter 2. The New Responsibility of Storm Survivors / 119

Chapter 3. The New Assurance for Storm Survivors / 122
    Authors Comments / 127

Section 1

Preparing for the Storm

35 On the same day, when evening had come, He said to them, "Let us cross over to the other side." 36 Now when they had left the multitude, they took Him along in the boat as He was. And other little boats were also with Him. 37 And a great windstorm arose, and the waves beat into the boat, so that it was already filling. 38 But He was in the stern, asleep on a pillow. And they awoke Him and said to Him, "Teacher, do You not care that we are perishing?"

39 Then He arose and rebuked the wind, and said to the sea, "Peace, be still!" And the wind ceased and there was a great calm. 40 But He said to them, "Why are you so fearful? How is it that you have no faith?" 41 And they feared exceedingly, and said to one another, "Who can this be, that even the wind and the sea obey Him!"

(Mark 4:35-41 nkjv)

Storm Preparation

From 2000 to 2010 I served as a pastor in a small community in the northeastern corner of North Carolina. Edenton was just an hour from the Outer Banks of North Carolina on the tip of the Albemarle Sound, just off the Atlantic Ocean. Soon after moving there from the safety of the mountains in Western North Carolina, I began to hear about Hurricanes. They spoke of "Hurricane Parties" and days spent indoors while the Hurricanes would howl and tear up the place. Coming from the mountains which tended to protect us from these storms our family was fascinated and intrigued at their stories.

In September of 2003 the National Weather Service started warning the Atlantic Coast about a tropical storm that had developed and had picked up enough steam to get the name Isabel. I learned when they get a name it's not a good thing. Soon all the local news stations began to put out information on storm preparedness. Brochures where available in grocery stores, hardware stores, convenience stores and even banks to let you know what you needed to do to prepare for the storm.

As Isabel moved across the Atlantic and Caribbean, the trackers of storm patterns began to predict that she would make landfall somewhere on the Carolina coastline. The authorities began to ask people to evacuate or at least make plans for a major hit.

I hate to say it but the Bishop's were somewhat excited. I realize now that it was a little naïve but we where planning for our "Hurricane Party." We had decided instead of evacuating and heading to stay with our family in the mountains that we would "ride it out" and play board games and eat junk food.

I did half-heartedly do some of the things listed on the "Storm Preparedness" brochures. I made sure I had fresh batteries in the flashlights. I bought some extra candles and matches, saved some water in empty milk jugs and put ice in some coolers I had. I made sure my cell phone was charged up and dug out an old transistor radio I hadn't used in years. I even filled up the bath-tub with water but had no idea why they had suggested this. I turned the kids trampoline upside down, and put the porch furniture in the storage building. I did all this thinking all this was over-kill and a waste of time.

Isabel made a direct hit on Hatteras Island in the Outer Banks on September 18th 2003. A new inlet was formed on Hatteras Island dubbed Isabel inlet, and she rode straight up the Albemarle Sound to hit Edenton around noon that day. I learned a lot about hurricanes and myself over the next few days.

1. I will pay close attention to the evacuation routes and run for the hills if it ever happens again.
2. You can fail to be prepared for a storm, but you can never be over prepared for a storm

Looking at the storm at sea story in Mark chapter 4, let's notice the most important way to be prepared for the storms of life.

Chapter 1

The Unique Opportunity
for Fellowship

Fellowship to most church folks means something involved with fried chicken and covered dish meals together. In the scripture the word means a bit more. In John's 1st epistle he speaks of us walking in fellowship with God.

> *If we say that we have fellowship with Him, and walk*
> *in darkness, we lie and do not practice the truth.*
> *But if we walk in the light as He is in the light, we*
> *have fellowship with one another, and the blood of*
> *Jesus Christ His Son cleanses us from all sin.*
> **(1 John 1:6-7 nkjv)**

The Greek word for fellowship has been taught and preached about a lot. The word is Koinonia and simply means communion or sharing in common.

John is not encouraging the believers to have fried chicken with God but to have communion with Him. The word communion is a compound word from the words common union. John is instructing us to have a union with God through the one that we have in common, Jesus and His work on the cross. The work of the cross satisfies God's demands for sin as well as our demand for our sin, the blood of Christ. The fellowship we have with the Father is based not upon our ability to be sinless but on the blood of Christ forgiving our sins as required by a Holy God.

When we celebrate communion at church we are celebrating the fact that the broken body and shed blood of Jesus Christ is the basis of our communion or common union with God. The broken body and shed blood of Jesus is what God's Holiness demands for our sin and what our sin requires. We are remembering Jesus and His work at bridging the gap between the Father's Holiness and our sinfulness. Because of Jesus we have fellowship with God. That is why I John chapter 1 goes on to speak of our confession of sin and chapter two speaks of Christ's advocacy and propitiation for us.

However my simple definition of the word fellowship is seen in this passage in Mark 4. A simple definition for fellowship is "two fellows in the same ship." A term that is used when you find someone going through some of the same storms as you are in life, "we seem to be in the same boat." That's fellowship when you share life together and go through the same things together.

I seem to find fellowship with pastors because I have served 25 years as a pastor. My wife and I have a unique fellowship with parents because we have 5 children. Now we are enjoying finding fellowship with grandparents because we are basking in the joys of grandparenthood.

Jesus has been speaking to the multitudes by the sea as was often His pulpit of choice in the gospels. This was probably due to the acoustical advantage of the wind coming off the sea carrying His voice.

Here in the passage in Mark we find after speaking to the multitudes Jesus gives an invitation,

> **On the same day, when evening had come, He said
> to them, "Let us cross over to the other side."**
>
> **(Mark 4:35)**

This offers a unique opportunity to be in the boat with Jesus. They could find themselves going where He's going and sharing the vessel with the great Rabbi.

Something I want you notice, are the three responses to this special invitation.

> ***Now when they had left the multitude, they
> took Him along in the boat as He was. And
> other little boats were also with Him.***
>
> **(Mark 4:35-36)**

The multitude, apparently, just went back home. They had things to do, and lives to live. They liked the things He was saying, at least some of them did. They were probably hoping He'd perform some miracle, there were rumors He was capable of that. But they were much too preoccupied with their own lives to follow Him.

A small number, the number is not given, got into the boat with Jesus and proceeded to launch out with Him to the other side. They would let Him navigate, tell them where to go and when to get there. They were turning their boats and their lives over to Him.

The last group I want you to notice is less in number than the multitude, but greater in number than those in the boat with Jesus, they chose to follow Him in their own "little boats". They were what we might call curious. They wanted to follow Him to see if there was anything to this man Jesus. Maybe He had some of what today is called, "paparazzi." They wanted to report every activity of this new rabbi that had came on the scene. We know that later in His ministry, possibly even this early, there were Pharisee's, scribes and other religious leaders from Jerusalem that were hoping to catch Him doing something to discredit His ministry.

So we see Jesus inviting all to go with Him to the other side but the responses vary. The same opportunity is offered today.

> ²⁰ ***Behold, I stand at the door and knock. If anyone
> hears My voice and opens the door, I will come in
> to him and dine with him, and he with Me.***
>
> **(Revelation 3:20)**

This invitation in Revelation is made to individual's to come open the door of fellowship with Jesus.

We find this same response to Christ's invitation for a relationship in people today. The multitude chooses to ignore His invitation and go on with their lives unaffected. A few choose to enter into a relationship with Him, guided and led by Him, going where He chooses and enjoying the closeness of the Savior.

> *"Enter by the narrow gate; for wide is the gate and broad is the way that leads to destruction, and there are many who go in by it. 14 Because narrow is the gate and difficult is the way which leads to life, and there are few who find it.*
> **(Matthew 7:13-14)**

We find that the majority of church folks today, are more like the "little boat" folks. They want to follow Jesus and go to heaven where He is. They just don't want to get too close for fear that on their way to the other side they may want to take some detours. They want to go a way they choose, that He may not wish to go. Everybody wants to go to heaven, the thing is, most of us just want to choose our own path. It's really not just about the destination, it is about the journey and the fact that for all of us the journey will include some storms.

The greatest thing we can do to prepare for the storms that may come is to have close fellowship with Jesus. A close personal relationship with Him is the greatest need when the storm hits. To have a prayer life, to have a practical knowledge of His Word and His ways and to have a relationship with the family of God is essential for weathering the storms of life as we will see as we look further.

Chapter 2

The Unexpected Occasion of a Storm

> *37 And a great windstorm arose, and the waves beat into the boat, so that it was already filling. 38 But He was in the stern, asleep on a pillow. And they awoke Him and said to Him, "Teacher, do You not care that we are perishing?"*
>
> **(Mark 4:37-38)**

When I was a young boy in Sunday School, I loved "Sunday School" songs. Songs like "Jesus Loves Me", "This Little Light of Mine" and "The B-I-B-L-E". I find myself often singing these songs still. I sing them to my grand-children. I even just sing them to myself in worship of God. They seem to just stick with you and make the message simple yet profound.

One of my favorite of these "Sunday School" songs, because it involved some hand motions, was "The Wise Man Built His House Upon the Rock". This song comes from an illustration Jesus used to close and apply His Sermon on the Mount.

²⁴ *"Therefore whoever hears these sayings of Mine, and does them, I will liken him to a wise man who built his house on the rock:* ²⁵ *and the rain descended, the floods came, and the winds blew and beat on that house; and it did not fall, for it was founded on the rock.*

²⁶ *"But everyone who hears these sayings of Mine, and does not do them, will be like a foolish man who built his house on the sand:* ²⁷ *and the rain descended, the floods came, and the winds blew and beat on that house; and it fell. And great was its fall."*

(Matthew 7:24-27)

My favorite part of this song was at the end when the rain came down, and the floods came up and the house on the sand went "Splattt." All the boys would shout loud enough to irritate the old ladies Bible study class down the hall, and clap our hands, stomp our feet in unison at the word "splatt."

You may have sung it differently because I'm sure there are different versions but that was the way we did it at the chagrin of the old ladies Bible study.

Jesus uses this illustration to emphasis the teachings that He had shared in His sermon, and the fact that those who applied these truths of His Kingdom would endure the rain like a house built on the rock, but those who ignored these truths would not endure the rain and their lives would fall. "Splatt"

The common theme in this story is the fact that either way it rained. If you build your house on the rock, it's going to rain. If your build your house on the sand, it's going to rain. It's a fact Longfellow brought out in his poem, "into every life some rain must fall" with the emphasis on "every life".

After riding out Hurricane Isabel my family stayed around a couple of days observing the devastating effects it had on our community. I finally sent my wife and children to the mountains to stay with her parents. The stored up water runs out quickly when several people are using the facilities.

After my family left, I volunteered to work at the local National Guard Armory by taking information on the needs of the multitude of people needing assistance, food, shelter, and to file for FEMA to help cover losses. The thing that touched me most was how the storm had put everyone on equal plains. The wealthy affluent that lived in beautiful waterfront homes stood in the same lines with those that lived in the "poor" part of town in the rundown buildings and projects. Storms are no respecter of persons.

Regardless of where you are in your walk of faith, regardless of your spiritual, economic or social standing, storms come. The storm came to those in the boat and in fellowship with Jesus and the same storm affected those in the little boats. It came unexpectedly and it came without respect.

It doesn't matter if you go to church every time the doors are open or if you're what I call a "ChrEaster" who only comes to church on Christmas and Easter, if you pray daily or rarely, if you can quote scripture or have never read your Bible, storms come.

Doctors say cancer or inoperable to the just and the unjust. As a pastor with responsibility to visit hospitals and preach funerals I have visited the wicked and the saints. I have preached funerals for those that I couldn't believed lived so long with their sinful lifestyles and for those that I couldn't explain why they suffered so young with a holy lifestyle.

Bosses say cut backs, lay-offs, or dismissed. In the difficult economic times we are in as a nation my heart has broken seeing hard working, devoted Christian husbands and fathers trying to figure out how they are going to support their families.

Mates say it's over, I don't love you anymore or there's someone else. Have you ever looked in the eyes of the husband or wife that thought the marriage was doing fine? Then they find out about the affair and their life is crushed and the storm blows in on what they thought was a bright spot in their life.

Schools or law officers call concerning your child. Children of good parents that have raised them in church and were at all their school functions have suffered the pain of a prodigal child. I have studied the story of the prodigal son and cannot find anything the prodigal's father did that was bad. Yet the storm that comes from loving our children hits our home too. My wife and I along with many good parents have asked that question, "Where did we go wrong," as a result of prodigals.

Many more scenarios can happen on an otherwise sunny day and suddenly the dark clouds block out the sun and it's hard to believe you can survive. These things happen regardless of where we are in our walk with God.

No doubt storms will come. The question is, how will we respond to the storm? Can we survive the storms that are inevitably going to come into our lives with our faith still intact? In our text we are only told of the response of those that were in the boat with Jesus, and it wasn't very "spiritual".

They questioned His actions, *"and He was in the stern, asleep on a pillow, and they awoke Him".* He should not be sleeping at a time like this, they were in trouble and what was He doing? Sleeping? We're going to fix that right now. We're going to wake Him up and let Him know what's going on. He needs to be informed of the situation here. How often do our prayer lives in the sudden storms involve crying out to God in desperate attempts to inform Him of our situations? Does God need information from us?

They questioned His care, **"Teacher, do you not care"** He is doing nothing to fix our problem. He doesn't care anything about us. We are just pawns in His kingdom agenda and we are expendable. Some well meaning brother or sister will come along and remind us of Romans 8:28, and another will be like one of Jobs friends after he lost his children, possessions, and health and encourage us to confess the sin in our lives. But the question in our minds is, "Does God even care what I'm going through here?"

They questioned His power to save them, *"that we are perishing"* (possibly a bit exaggerated). He doesn't care and He is just going to let this storm destroy us they thought. When the storm is raging often we think this is the one that will destroy me.

Not such a "spiritual" response from the people closest to Jesus in the storm, however I find some encouragement from this because I have the same tendencies in my storms. To doubt that He's doing anything and that I must inform Him. To question His love for me that He would even allow me to go through this. To feel I offered my boat and followed His leadership and this is what I get for it. We often start making a mental list of all the things we have done for Him at church and now can't believe He's letting this happen to us.

The only response to the storm that is recorded is negative, defeated surrender to circumstances, and it does not shed a good light on people in fellowship with Jesus in a storm. We are all guilty of having great faith when the sun is shining but displaying a gloomy pessimism when the storms roll in.

However, I think there is one great thing about these "same boat" disciples. They knew where Jesus was and knew how to get to Him because they had a close relationship to Him. They were scared. They doubted a lot of things, but when the going got rough, they knew who to turn to and how to get there.

Being in fellowship with Jesus will not prevent storms, nor will it assure our response will be to sing praise songs like Paul and Silas did in prison. But it will assure that we know where He is and how to get to Him.

We are not told of how the other groups responded, so I want to take some liberties here and speculate on what might have been their response.

The multitude that had ignored His invitation for fellowship hunkered down in their self-made houses and used this to protect them from the storm. Still today the people that ignore His invitation hunker in their self-made defenses to hide from the storms. Addictions, immoral lifestyles, lusts and materialism is what the world uses today to hide from the storms that inevitably hit us all. Instead of dealing with storms and learning and growing from them, they escape in hopes the storm will quickly pass. One song writer said, "I do not know how others make it through, that do not go to Calvary as I do."

I have had people come to me while going through a storm asking for my help. When they come they let me know they are not "church people" and don't want me to quote Bible verses. They just want me to help them know how to deal with their current stormy situation. I tell them quickly that I have no answer other than the Bible and faith in Christ.

The folks I really want to speculate on based upon 25 years as a pastor are the "little boat" followers of Jesus. I believe they followed at a safe distance while the seas where calm but as the wind picked up and things got harrowing they attempted to get closer to His boat. They began to row desperately and cry out, "Hey Jesus, can we get in the boat with You?" They probably began to bargain with Him, "If you let me in the boat and fix this storm, I'll come hear you speak every time, I'll even contribute regularly to your cause. Just help us get through this storm, and we'll do anything."

This is just speculation on my part but I've seen it many times in church work. We've all watched the folks that half-heartedly come to church with little true devotion. Then a child gets sick, they lose their job, or a storm of another source rages into their lives and they want to make commitments and develop a prayer life. They start reading their Bibles and are calling the preacher whom they have avoided talking to for years when the seas were calm.

The greatest way to increase fellowship with Jesus is a storm; after the terrorist attacks of September 11 in 2001 church attendance, prayer vigils and people attempting to get in the boat with Jesus increased. One of the local public schools invited myself and other pastors to come to their schools and meet with students in a room that had been temporarily set aside as a prayer room. Remember staff cannot lead a child in prayer in public schools. It's not the staff's fault but the government. However after the storm of 9/11 the government that forbids prayer in schools turned its head and welcomed any attempt to get in the boat with Jesus.

The time to develop a prayer life is before the storm. The time to grow in understanding God's word is before the storm. The time to build and grow close in a relationship with Christ is before the storm. So that when it hits, we can know where He is, who He is, and how to get to Him.

Why should we begin to build a close fellowship with Jesus? Because it's gonna rain, and you can never be over prepared for a storm.

Chapter 3

The Unquestionable Object of Faith

³⁹ Then He arose and rebuked the wind, and said to the sea, "Peace, be still!" And the wind ceased and there was a great calm. ⁴⁰ But He said to them, "Why are you so fearful? How is it that you have no faith?" ⁴¹ And they feared exceedingly, and said to one another, "Who can this be, that even the wind and the sea obey Him!"

(Mark 4:39-41)

I have a little warped eschatological hope that in eternity we all get remote controls or at least the men do. We all know women can't understand remote controls. (Just kidding ladies) These remotes will allow us to go to a replay of Biblical events and see it (maybe even in slow motion). I have no scripture to back this up, so just humor me. I would love to see the expressions on the faces and the responses of people involved, to the acts of God in the scripture.

This scene is one I would choose to replay, and replay again and again like I do Andy Griffin episodes. After they woke Jesus, from where He was sleeping, was He aggravated like I am when someone wakes me from a nap?

Did He simply walk to some point at the boat and rebuke it as if to say, "Wind you be quiet, I'm trying to get some sleep"? Did He then shake His head and speak to His followers in the boat with Him about their lack of faith and then lay back down to finish His nap, while they sat with their mouth open and chins hitting the ground in awe of what He did? Wouldn't you like to see the details of how that played out?

What we do have is a description of how this demonstration of power affected those who had chosen to be in fellowship with Jesus and the lesson they learned from the storm.

Before we discuss the men in fellowship with Jesus let's consider what the others learned from this storm that suddenly came into their lives and then suddenly left. Again, I am just speculating with no comment from scripture.

I feel sure the multitudes at home as well as the little boat followers where equally relieved when the storm that threatened their normal lives subsided. Probably they were thankful that it passed so quickly but not really sure who to thank. They probably didn't learn a lot or grow from the experience, but they sure felt "lucky".

How often have we gone through storms that terrorized us and that we thought would destroy us and then it was over. We have had the threat of some health issue and then it got better, or the doctor said he was wrong or it didn't show up on the new X-ray. We found another job, or the kids started doing better. They decided to work on the marriage or saw a good counselor who helped them work through some issues.

We say things like; "That medicine the doctor prescribed really helped." "That counselor or even the pastor really helped our problems". "We sure were lucky that the money came in or that job came open".

Truth is all of our storms are calmed by the one whom even the wind and the sea, obey, but if we are not in fellowship with Him when the storm comes, we fail to realize the extent of His power when He heals or provides and moves in our life. He doesn't get the full glory, and we never learn anything of Him and His power. Luck and professionals get more of the praise than He does, and we chalk it up to coincidence.

But those who were in the boat with Jesus, those who had fellowship with Him knew this wasn't luck or coincidence. I don't think He made this a great spectacular event. He simply rebuked the wind and sea, and they obeyed Him. The result of what they experienced because of their close proximity to the Son of God, forever changed what they believed about Him.

In the Greek language there are three words that are translated "fear" in the New Testament. One is a bad negative fear which means cowardly. The next is more positive and means awed or amazed. The best fear is where we get our word eulogy and means devotion or life changing.

In this passage two of these three words are used. When Jesus asked them, "***Why are you so <u>fearful</u>***", He was attributing to them the worst most negative kind of fear. He was calling them cowards which is the opposite of faith. Later when the fellow boaters watched Him rebuke the wind and sea and saw the result, it says they "***<u>feared</u> exceedingly***." This was a more positive fear this fear was a sense of awe and amazement at the power and authority of Jesus.

The men in the boat and in fellowship with Jesus that stormy night did not grow in their understanding of storms and why they happen. They did not grow in their ability to overcome the devastation of a storm and how to escape it. They grew in the realization of who Jesus was and replied, "Who can this be" the Old King James version says, "What manner of man is this?"

These men grew in their faith not in themselves, not in luck or circumstances, not even in understanding why storms come. They grew in the realization that whatever storm comes into their lives this man, who is no ordinary man, can speak into that storm and calm the winds and waves. Their lives would never be the same because before the storm ever hit, they were in fellowship with Jesus and now they were amazed at His power.

How about you? Are you in fellowship with Him? Do you have a prayer life and a practical understanding of His Word? If a storm enters your life tomorrow, will you need to struggle to get to Him or are you already in a relationship with Him?

It's going to rain! Are you prepared for the next storm?

Section 1 – Preparing for the Storm – Think it out

In the first section we discussed the fact that storms come into our lives unexpectedly. Things may be sailing along smoothly and then suddenly things go bad. This can happen at any time to anyone. The greatest way to be prepared for these storms is to be in "fellowship" with Christ before it comes.

Scriptural Reading - I John 1:5 – 2:2

> *This is the message which we have heard from Him and declare to you, that God is light and in Him is no darkness at all. ⁶ If we say that we have fellowship with Him, and walk in darkness, we lie and do not practice the truth. ⁷ But if we walk in the light as He is in the light, we have fellowship with one another, and the blood of Jesus Christ His Son cleanses us from all sin.*
>
> *⁸ If we say that we have no sin, we deceive ourselves, and the truth is not in us. ⁹ If we confess our sins, He is faithful and just to forgive us our sins and to cleanse us from all unrighteousness. ¹⁰ If we say that we have not sinned, we make Him a liar, and His word is not in us.*
>
> *2 My little children, these things I write to you, so that you may not sin. And if anyone sins, we have an Advocate with the Father, Jesus Christ the righteous. ² And He Himself is the propitiation for our sins, and not for ours only but also for the whole world.*

Discussion Questions:

John declares in this short epistle that God is light, and later that God is love. In order for us to be in fellowship with Him we must walk in light and not in darkness. God will not come into fellowship or ride in the boat with us if we are sailing in darkness or sin.

1. Does this mean that we must be perfectly sinless before God can have fellowship with us? Is that even possible?
2. Verse 8 makes it clear if we deny we have sin we are liars to others and ourselves. How can we have fellowship with the God of light if we are often walking in darkness?

John goes on to speak of the blood of Jesus cleansing us from sin, and the faithfulness of God in forgiving our sins if we confess our sins. In Chapter 2 He reminds us that Jesus serves as our advocate and the propitiation or "satisfying sacrifice" for our sins.

3. What does the blood of Jesus, confession and the advocacy of Christ have to do with our fellowship with God?
4. Is this passage speaking about eternity and heaven or hell or is it speaking about our daily walk and fellowship with God?

Section 2

Finding Peace in the Storm

⁴⁵ Immediately He made His disciples get into the boat and go before Him to the other side, to Bethsaida, while He sent the multitude away. ⁴⁶ And when He had sent them away, He departed to the mountain to pray. ⁴⁷ Now when evening came, the boat was in the middle of the sea; and He was alone on the land. ⁴⁸ Then He saw them straining at rowing, for the wind was against them. Now about the fourth watch of the night He came to them, walking on the sea, and would have passed them by. ⁴⁹ And when they saw Him walking on the sea, they supposed it was a ghost, and cried out; ⁵⁰ for they all saw Him and were troubled. But immediately He talked with them and said to them, "Be of good cheer! It is I; do not be afraid." ⁵¹ Then He went up into the boat to them, and the wind ceased. And they were greatly amazed in themselves beyond measure, and marveled. ⁵² For they had not understood about the loaves, because their heart was hardened.

Mark 6:45-52

Tracking the Storm

In 2003 when hurricane Isabel came raging through our small town I had done some of the things suggested in the Storm Preparedness brochures. I had batteries, flashlights and candles in preparation for the power outage that was predicted. I had found an old transistor radio and put in fresh batteries to keep up with what was happening. I also had charged up my cell phone and even an extra battery for it, to keep communication with people outside of our town.

Sure enough, the power went out very early into the storm, and the only way to keep up with what was happening was to listen to the radio. However when the nearest radio station's tower was hit and it went off the air, I was riding blind. The old transistor radio didn't have a lot of range and ended up useless.

My brother who lives in the mountains in western North Carolina, called my cell phone to check on us, and he became my lifeline. He works with computers as a career and always has access to one. He began to track the storm on-line and give me regular updates on how it was moving throughout the day.

It cleared up at one point and we went outside to see the damage. I called and told him it had passed and we were fine. He said "brother, don't go far from the house, according to the radar, the eye of the storm is over you right now, but the worst is coming from the tail of the storm". He was correct; the back end of Isabel was more ferocious than the front end.

Somehow I managed to find some peace with the fact that I had a contact that helped me understand what the storm was doing, how long it was going to last, and how much damage it was doing.

Unfortunately in regard to the storms of life there is no Doppler radar, no storm trackers to warn us what category the storm is, when or where it will hit, and how long it will last. We go through these storms of life blind, hanging on, begging God to calm the storm and not sure what He's doing.

Song writers write about peace in the storm, and shelter in the time of storms, but often this peace is hard to find. I think the reason we have a hard time finding peace in the storm is that we demand answers. We feel if we can just wrap our head around it and get an understanding of the storm, we will find peace.

We want to know why? What did we do to deserve this? How long will we have to endure it? When there's a lull, is it over or is it going to get worse?

I have learned if we spend our energy trying to understand and track our storms, we will simply run out of energy. If the only way we will find peace is to understand the storm, we will never find peace.

Go with me to a new storm at sea story in Mark chapter 6 to learn some things about finding peace in the storms of life.

Chapter 4

Often God's Purposes are Hard to Understand in the Storm

Chapter 6 of Mark is filled with what might be called some political masterpieces. The followers of Jesus do not completely understand His kingdom and what He is building, but they are committed to being a part of it. Some of them have become His self appointed campaign managers, attempting to advise Him and make sure He does all the things necessary to be elected. They fail to understand that He is not trying to win the majority vote, He is already the King of His Kingdom and carrying out His Kingdom agenda.

However they are pleased with the way things are going. As the chapter opens up He has empowered them with power over sickness and unclean spirits and sent them out two by two into the villages around them to do miracles in His name. This was a tremendous success and has created a great name for the King and the campaign.

King Herod has cut off the head of John the Baptist which has stirred up the people in the region, and Herod's approval ratings are dropping fast.

They come back together to report about the campaign tour and are excited about the way they were used to win the people with this power to heal. Jesus suggest they take a break, go on a retreat to the other side of the sea.

> *30 Then the apostles gathered to Jesus and told Him all things, both what they had done and what they had taught. 31 And He said to them, "Come aside by yourselves to a deserted place and rest a while." For there were many coming and going, and they did not even have time to eat. 32 So they departed to a deserted place in the boat by themselves.*
>
> **(Mark 6:30-32)**

Then as the multitudes, impressed by this man Jesus, come to where the disciples and Jesus have slipped off for a little R&R, Jesus sits them down and begins to teach.

> *33 But the multitudes saw them departing, and many knew Him and ran there on foot from all the cities. They arrived before them and came together to Him. 34 And Jesus, when He came out, saw a great multitude and was moved with compassion for them, because they were like sheep not having a shepherd. So He began to teach them many things.*
>
> **(Mark 6:33-34)**

The disciples are tired and really want to begin the retreat and noting that it's getting late, they advise Jesus to send the people away so they can eat.

> *35 When the day was now far spent, His disciples came to Him and said, "This is a deserted place, and already the hour is late. 36 Send them away, that they may go into the surrounding country and villages and buy themselves bread; for they have nothing to eat."*
>
> **(Mark 6:35-36)**

I seriously doubt the disciples were too deeply concerned with the people's hunger but simply were ready to rest. The scripture says Jesus was moved with compassion for the multitude, but I don't think the disciples were, based upon the rest of the story.

> *37 But He answered and said to them, "You give them something to eat." And they said to Him, "Shall we go and buy two hundred denarii worth of bread and give them something to eat?"*
>
> **(Mark 6:37)**

However the next thing Jesus does is political genius. He feeds five thousand men, plus women and children with five loaves of bread and two fish. (This is another one of those scenes I hope to use my remote to see replayed.) Imagine the expressions on their faces as this plays out. From what we are told, I think their expressions went from disagreement of the idea, to confusion at what was happening, to complete laughter as they kept serving thousands and thousands were fed.

> *38 But He said to them, "How many loaves do you have? Go and see."And when they found out they said, "Five, and two fish." 39 Then He commanded them to make them all sit down in groups on the green grass. 40 So they sat down in ranks, in hundreds and in fifties. 41 And when He had taken the five loaves and the two fish, He looked up to heaven, blessed and broke the loaves, and gave them to His disciples to set before them; and the two fish He divided among them all. 42 So they all ate and were filled. 43 And they took up twelve baskets full of fragments and of the fish. 44 Now those who had eaten the loaves were about five thousand men.*
>
> **(Mark 6:38-44)**

I'm sure it crossed their mind this is the epitome of political genius, feeding people for free. Admit it; if a politician were to do this feat today, it would be a shoe-in for votes.

They became excited with what had been accomplished the last few days; Herod's popularity slipping and now this. They could invade the palace now and take over.

Instead Jesus begins to send the multitude away with full bellies and makes His disciples get in the boat and head back home while He stays to pray. No riots in front of the palace, no planning the campaign, they don't even get to finish the retreat.

> *45 Immediately He made His disciples get into the boat and go before Him to the other side, to Bethsaida, while He sent the multitude away. 46 And when He had sent them away, He departed to the mountain to pray.*
>
> **(Mark 6:45-46)**

Verse 45 says He *"made them"* get in the boat. This implies compelled, strongly urged against their will or desires.

Sometimes what He asks us to do just doesn't make sense. We think we know His agenda but it is actually our agenda and He asks us to do something that doesn't fit our agenda.

Anyone who has walked in fellowship with God for any time has at one time or another been asked or compelled by God to do something that did not fit logically. Maybe He has led you to give when it was not logical to give. To speak when you would have rather remained silent or moved on you to remain silent when you would have rather spoken. Maybe He has moved on your heart and circumstances to leave when you thought everything was fine and would rather stay, or He said stay when everything was falling apart and you would love to run away. Anyone who has truly sought God and attempted to obey Him has been called upon to do things they don't really understand.

That is why scriptures remind us that *"His ways are not our ways"* and *"His ways are past finding out"* (or understanding). The often quoted Proverb speaks of wisdom as learning to *"Trust in the Lord with all your heart"* and then I think the big challenge is next, *"And lean not to your own understanding"*.

We will never find peace in going on a quest to understand what God is doing in our lives because often we will never understand. That's why we must trust.

As we look further into the Mark 6 storm, we will find this instruction to His disciples even harder to understand because not only did they not want to leave because of what had taken place. They find He leads them straight into a storm. Not only was His guidance confusing based upon the past events, it got even harder to understand due to what He had led them into.

In 1985 I was a 25 year old "preacher boy" fresh out of Bible College with a burning desire to "get a church". In the qualifications for a bishop in I Timothy 3 it states that, ***"If a man desires the position of a bishop, he desires a good work"***. After 25 years now of doing it, I find myself wanting to get a better Greek definition of that word "good work," but when I was 25 years old having served as a youth pastor for several years and having spent some time as an interim supply pastor, I felt certain I was ready to serve as a Sr. Pastor. I was seeking God to guide and provide me with this opportunity.

I came in contact with a small group of people wanting to establish and build a church in a community in the upstate of South Carolina. I began to preach for them on Sunday's in a rented store front building and establish a relationship with them. As I prayed and they prayed, God gave His approval to us all that I would be their pastor. I felt certain as did they that God had put us together, but the day they voted me in as pastor made us all second guess.

I had spent a sleepless night that Saturday night with a headache. I put it off on the excitement of the next day. The people that had formed the Lakeview Baptist Church were going to vote on me as their pastor. I was going to get the first Sr. Pastor role of my ministry if the vote went my way.

That morning I was sick, headache, vomiting and chalked it up to nerves. I preached a very weak message, and they called the congregation into conference to vote on me as their pastor. They asked me to leave the service, and wait on the results. My wife and I went out to the parking lot and sat in the car praying. They came out and asked me to come back in and announced that the vote was 100% to call me to be their first pastor. There was a lot of shaking hands, hugging necks and joy.

To make a long story short, a few hours later I was hospitalized with spinal meningitis and quarantined from even my wife. They asked for the names of everyone I had been in contact with over the past 24 hours. (Remember the shaking hands and hugging necks) It was a nightmare. The next few days were a blur of excruciating pain, heavy medications and in and out of consciousness.

As I recuperated from the meningitis, I asked a lot of whys. Had I missed it? Had God lead me straight into that storm? I still don't understand why and probably never will understand why God allowed that at that time. I do know that the next 14 years we saw God's hand move in people's lives and bless the wonderful ministry of Lakeview Baptist Church in Pickens, SC.

When Jesus made His disciples get on that boat and head to the other side, He went on the mountain to pray. Was He praying for a storm? No doubt He's God and knew it was coming. Instead of protecting them from it and encouraging them not to go because it looks like another storm is coming, He made them go into it.

Does God use the storms? Does God send the storms? How can we understand it? Are we expected to try and understand it?

If to have peace in the storm, we must understand the purposes of God in the storm we may never have peace because some of His ways are past finding out.

Chapter 5

Often God's Timing is
Hard to Understand

Every good Christian Book store that sales Christian paraphernalia will have a plaque, banner or picture for sale with an eagle soaring in the clouds and this quote from the prophet Isaiah:

> *³¹ But those who wait on the Lord Shall renew their strength;*
>
> *They shall mount up with wings like eagles,*
> *They shall run and not be weary,*
>
> *They shall walk and not faint.*
>
> **Isaiah 40:31**

Isaiah has been warning Israel that the storm of God's chastisement is coming but that they must wait upon the Lord. Something that seems to be a theme throughout the Bible concerning our relationship with God is the act of waiting and everyone knows the waiting room is not our favorite place.

It's everywhere! Promises are attached to those who wait upon the Lord. Commands are made to wait upon the Lord. Songs are sung about waiting. The problem is as humans we just hate the waiting room.

If we have an appointment at noon, we show up at 11:59 so we don't have to wait. (Unless you're like my wife who shows up at 12:05 so that others have to wait.) A country song came out a couple of years ago called "Waiting on a Woman." It has become one of my life songs because I have done a lot of that for the past 31 years.

When we are on time and then are told to wait, we get frustrated and keep looking at our watch. If we go to a restaurant and sit down, we want the waitress to come quickly, get our drink orders, get our orders and get the meal out quickly even if we have nowhere to be. If we are at a traffic light and the person in front of us doesn't take off immediately when the light turns green, we honk the horn to get them moving. We don't like to wait.

This creates a real problem in a walk with God who sees a day as a thousand years and requires that we wait. This waiting becomes especially difficult in a storm.

When Isabel hit, the initial front of the storm was a little eerie but interesting. As the wind picked up and continued to blow at 75 miles an hour making our old house whistle and moan it became more eerie. When it lasted for several hours it became nerve racking. Waiting for it to end, waiting for the sounds to die down waiting to see how much damage had been done left us all on edge after a while.

It's a fact: God's ways are not our ways, and His timing is not our timing. God created the sun by day and the moon by night for man to have time in his life and be able to manage their lives by time. God's clock is eternal and He is in all time. He is eternally content but man is on a clock.

These disciples who had obeyed Jesus and set out to sea to cross to the other side in obedience to Jesus had gotten to the middle of the sea, and a storm of wind began to fight against them. No matter how hard they would row, the term used is ***"straining at rowing,"*** the wind just wouldn't let them get anywhere.

Storms are like that, we fight to get forward, and they keep knocking us backward. We want to move on with life, but this health issue, or family problem, or financial pitfall keeps knocking us down, and we can't get anywhere.

But notice the time frame detailed in the story.

The days and nights were measured by what were called watches. There were four watches which came in three hour stints; the first watch of the night was from 6pm to 9pm; the second watch went from 9pm to 12am; the third watch from 12am to 3am; and the fourth watch of the night went from 3am until 6am. Then of course the day watches would begin for the same three hour intervals.

> *⁴⁷ Now when evening came, the boat was in the middle of the sea; and He was alone on the land. ⁴⁸ Then He saw them straining at rowing, for the wind was against them.*
> **(Mark 6:47-48a)**

That meant when the evening watches had began around 6pm they were half way across. I have read somewhere that the time it took to cross the Sea of Galilee in that day was maybe an hour and a half to two hours at the most. These guys should have gotten home in time for dinner and the late news. Note, however, how long they were there in the middle of the sea straining and rowing against a storm. Then notice how long they were left in the storm fighting against it.

> *Now about the fourth watch of the night He came to them*
> **(Mark 6:48b)**

The fourth watch! They should have been home by the end of the first watch easily and it was sometime after 3:00am before He came. Possibly the sun was getting ready to rise. They say it's always darkest before the dawn so they were there until the darkest part of the night and completely exhausted from straining and rowing before He came to them.

Sometimes it gets worse before it gets better.

Lifeguards at the beach are trained that if they are ever faced with a person drowning and fighting to survive, they must wait until they quit fighting to save them, or they could drag you under. I could not imagine just waiting while they were drowning.

That seems to be what Jesus was doing. Waiting until they came to the place they could not save themselves and then He came to them. Maybe that's what God's waiting room is all about. God has us wait until we are surrendered to Him; then He comes to us.

Often His timing is hard to understand.

So, He finally comes to them to help them in their storm, but He doesn't just rebuke the wind and tell it to "cut it out and behave" like He did before. This time even the way He comes is hard to understand.

Chapter 6

Often God's Answers are
Hard to Understand

*...He came to them, walking on the sea, and would have
passed them by. ⁴⁹ And when they saw Him walking
on the sea, they supposed it was a ghost, and cried
out; ⁵⁰ for they all saw Him and were troubled.*

(Mark 6:48 – 50)

Most of you reading this book if asked, "Do you believe in ghost?"
would probably say no. Theologically or just as adults we all know
ghost stories are for children.

However place yourself in the middle of a raging sea. You've been
fighting the wind and waves for hours and are completely exhausted. It's
near morning, and you've had no sleep. Suddenly you look out over the
sea and see something coming. What is it? You and those in the boat with
you begin to point and debate. The sleepiness is gone as adrenalin begins
to rush in the acceptance that you're not just seeing things. There really is
something coming across the surface of the Sea of Galilee.

Is it a very small vessel? No way, their large boat has made no progress in this storm for hours; a smaller vessel wouldn't last five minutes in this kind of sea.

Is it a sea creature? Some Loch Ness Monster type creature that I'm sure they sat around the boat at night while fishing and told "ghost stories" about. I'm sure there were plenty of sea myth's in their day too. Maybe it's real?

As it gets closer, it begins to be obvious it has the form of a man and is obviously walking effortless across the sea. The only logical explanation is a ghost. I'm sure someone on the boat said it first. Somebody probably said, no way we don't believe in ghost. As it came closer, these hardened fishermen became believers…. in ghost.

Imagine yourself in your car at night on a dark dirt road out in the country. Suddenly your car just stops and the engine dies, the headlights go out and a bright light begins to beam down from the sky. You might try to make sense out of it, but eventually you would be convinced it's a UFO. Even if in the day, you deny believing in Alf. Isn't it amazing how we can believe or at least imagine the possibility of some myths like Loch Ness, Bigfoot, Alf (this ages me) and UFO's, but we have a hard time believing the Bible.

They had seen Jesus rebuke the wind and sea, and the raging wind and violent sea obeyed His voice and command. They had come to realize He was no mere man; although, I'm not sure they had come to know that He was deity. Why would they even think He could walk on water?

Storms if we go through them with Jesus are the only way I know to grow in our understanding of who He is, how much He loves us and His power in our lives. We may never understand our storms, the purpose and the timing, but we can grow to know Him more.

In Philippians 3:10 Paul said: ***that I may know Him and the power of His resurrection, and the fellowship of His sufferings, being conformed to His death,***

This seems to indicate that "knowing" Him in a greater way is directly connected to suffering and dying to our self confidence. Storms come and stay longer than we want for the purpose of teaching us that we can't go forward without Him.

The main point to notice here is that even when He does step into our stormy lives on our stormy seas, the answer is often as scary as the storm.

In 2003 a storm began to blow into my life in the area of health issues. It began with unexplainable body aches and weakness, and progressed to days of immobility and extreme pain. My local doctor was stumped and referred me to the University of North Carolina medical center. Through many trips to Chapel Hill, North Carolina, many hospital stays, and a barrage of test and poking and prodding, I was diagnosed with a rare degenerative disease called polymyositis. It is in the Muscular Dystrophy family, and it had taken a toll on my health. I went for weeks unable to preach at church, go to my kids ball games, and was simply homebound except for trips to the doctor.

The treatment for this was pain pills, an immune suppressant drug (which suppress your immune system and makes you vulnerable to all germs) and high doses of prednisone which in my opinion, had side effects that were worse than the disease itself. The dark clouds of depression hung over me and my mind was in constant confusion, as a result of the drugs I was taking. However God did step in and began to strengthen me and after several months of anxiety and some physical suffering, I began to be get a new limited degree of my life back. God was showing me what He had shown Paul in II Corinthians 12 concerning Paul's "thorn in the flesh."

⁹ And He said to me, "My grace is sufficient for you, for My strength is made perfect in weakness."

(II Corinthians 12:9)

As this storm began to dissipate what I didn't realize was that another one, that would be much more testing in our lives was building.

I have mentioned that my wife and I have five children. We have four sons and one daughter. I love my boys and find great joy in the relationship we share, but with only one daughter, I guess you can imagine the relationship I share with her. She is "daddy's girl", and has a special place in my heart. What I didn't know but learned later was the effect that my illness had on Megan my daughter. She became angry with God for making her daddy sick. As a result of this misplaced anger Megan began pulling away from us and changed her friends, her interest, and almost became someone we didn't recognize her senior year of high school.

We didn't realize the severity of these changes until she got in trouble at school for marijuana and was not allowed to play soccer her senior year. Soccer was her passion and she was very good at it, but as I mentioned her interests had changed.

She started dating a young man we did not approve of, he was in trouble with the law, and had been arrested more than once for illegal drug activity. When we tried to stop her we got the reply many parents get, "I'm eighteen and you can't stop me." This didn't stop us from trying but we didn't stop her from spiraling downward in her lifestyle.

One night Megan snuck out of the house and left a note on her bed telling us she had been busted for marijuana possession and could not face us with it. She had left and would be gone for the next several months.

The storm raged into our lives with sleepless nights, many tears and desperate cries to God for help. In the health storm I had gone through the church and entire community had encircled us and given support. In this personal family storm there were words of encouragement, but embarrassment and shame made us feel we were in this one alone.

Megan had moved in with the young man and we had no idea what she was doing and what she was involved in. I began to fight the storm cloud of hatred toward this young man, anger at my daughter, and tried to find a way to continue serving God as a pastor, give my boys the attention they needed and deserved, while being consumed with my daughters situation.

We prayed that God would bring our prodigal daughter back to us and after a few months He answered our prayers. Megan came back home, with legal issues to face and decisions to make. We realized quickly though, that just because she had come back home she was still distant and removed from us. The storm was not over just changing things around us.

Megan continued to see the young man, and then a few months after she had returned home we got a phone call from a law officer that Megan had been involved in an accident and the ambulance was bringing her to the hospital. We got to the scene of the accident before they left with her to find out what had happened. Megan had been ejected from a moving vehicle and was on the side of the road with a lot of pain from the impact.

When we got to the Emergency Room they began to do test and then the doctor told us something that at the time scared us to the degree that those disciples in the boat must have been. They needed to do more test but could not because our beautiful nineteen year old daughter was pregnant. Because she was so young, unmarried, and the father of the baby was a young man I not only disapproved of but had begun to despise, this was one of the scariest moments of my life.

The amazing thing was, that from that day my daughter began to come back to us. She began to talk and cry and repent of her lifestyle. She opened up during long middle of the night tearful talks about the drugs, the abuse she had endured. She shared how on one drug induced night, she had cried out to God, that she knew she needed out and didn't know how and had asked God to do whatever it took to get back to Him. She believes that was the night that her baby was conceived.

In September 2010 my first grandson was born, and as I cried and held him that day I realized that the dark clouds had left and the sun was shining. God had sent this baby, and I believe He gives all life and makes no mistakes, we sin but he comes walking into our messes and turns them into blessings. The thing that I feared, had been God's answer, and His way of walking into my storm and scaring me with His answer.

God may have sent the storm to wake us up, or to challenge us to leave something we are comfortable with. He may be calling us to live with pain and learn to walk in His strength. He may send the storm to teach us how to deal with hatred and forgiveness and the only way He could have gotten our attention to accept His answer was to put us in a situation where we just want the storm to end, and will accept His answer if He'll just calm the storm.

Now however Jesus has showed up and taken the disciples attention from the storm. It's not the storm that has them fearful now, it's the way Jesus came to them, what Jesus was doing was scaring them more than what the storm was doing.

These disciples, when coming to the conclusion that they were seeing a ghost cried out in fear.

I know I want to see this instant replay when I get my heavenly remote, a boat full of seasoned fishermen, hardened by the sea and hard work, now cowering in a boat together like grade school girls at a slumber party, screaming in fear. I would have never screamed like that, I know I wouldn't because I would have already fainted and been lying unconscious on the boat floor.

Often His answers are hard to understand.

Sometimes Jesus speaks to our storms and calms them

Sometime He lets the storm rage and calms us.

Chapter 7

Often We Never Understand
but We Grow

⁵¹ Then He went up into the boat to them, and the wind ceased. And they were greatly amazed in themselves beyond measure, and marveled.

(Mark 6:50-51)

God's ways in the storm are hard to understand. If it's simply for the purpose of making me grow, I'm ready. Teach me what I need to learn, and let's get over with this storm. I just want some peace, some fair weather and sunshine. I'm sick of this storm.

If you have ever spent any time speaking with men or women that have been incarcerated you know that the number one thing on their mind is getting out. When we are going through the storm we get consumed with the idea of getting out of the storm. However tired we get in the storm, we must come to the place that we realize God has sent or allowed the storm for a purpose, and begin to desire that the purpose of God be accomplished.

Let me emphasize that peace often must come in the heart before the wind dies down, and the storm ceases to rage. Peace is the objective, not changed circumstances. Peace in the midst of the storm is what we need to find.

My wife is an amazing woman, with strengths that I am constantly discovering, that I didn't know existed, even though we have been married over thirty three years.

When Hurricane Isabel hit, I have talked about the anxiety, excitement, phone calls to my brother reporting regularly, transistor radios and constantly looking out the window to note any new developments. My children and myself, were as antsy as a cat at a dog show, but guess what my wife did throughout the biggest part of the storm. She took the opportunity to catch up on her sleep. The biggest part of the storm hit in the middle of the day not at night. However, she realized she couldn't be multitasking, so she went in the bedroom and slept. It was rather aggravating to me. How could she sleep?

In the first section of the book on the Mark chapter four, storm we see aggravation in the disciples because Jesus slept through the storm, and Jesus aggravated that they woke Him to give Him a storm update. It was that way at the Bishop house during hurricane Isabel, I was aggravated that she was sleeping through it, and she was aggravated when I woke her to give her a report.

To become more like Jesus, we must learn to sleep through the storm. We must grow to realize some things that this story brings out. The first words of verse 48 occur not when Jesus was walking on the water to the disciples, but while He was on the mountain praying.

> **⁴⁸ *Then He saw them straining at rowing,***
> ***for the wind was against them***
>
> **Mark 6:48**

Peace comes when we come to accept that when the clouds in our lives are heavy, and we can't see God's hand, and can't understand what He's doing or where He is, He sees us.

The ultimate Biblical storm recorded in the Bible was the "big one" in Genesis. The flood that destroyed the earth and all that was in it except for Noah and his family on the Ark. When Noah came off the Ark, God made a covenant with Noah that included new dietary, governmental and worship laws.

In this covenant God promised Noah that never again would He use a flood to destroy the earth and placed the rainbow in the clouds to seal the covenant. I thought for years that this was to assure Noah during cloudy days, so he would remember the covenant and not be afraid. However I had a hard time with this because honestly when the cloud cover is heavy and the storm is bad, I can't see any rainbows.

Scientifically the rainbow is formed by the light of the Sun hitting the moisture and breaking the colors into a prism. When the cloud cover is heavy, the sun doesn't shine through and the rainbow doesn't appear. As a matter of fact, the appearance of rainbows is rather rare. I have seen some beautiful rainbows but not with every storm.

Then I went back to Genesis 9 and read it again,

> *13 I set My rainbow in the cloud, and it shall be for the sign of the covenant between Me and the earth. 14 It shall be, when I bring a cloud over the earth, that the rainbow shall be seen in the cloud; 15 and I will remember My covenant which is between Me and you and every living creature of all flesh; the waters shall never again become a flood to destroy all flesh. 16 The rainbow shall be in the cloud, and I will look on it to remember the everlasting covenant between God and every living creature of all flesh that is on the earth."*
> **(Genesis 9:13-16)**

Notice God does not tell Noah that when he sees the rainbow he can be reminded. He says, when I see the rainbow, I will remember. I will talk about this storm more in the last section of the book.

Sometimes when the clouds in our lives are heavy, we cannot see the sun. There is no rainbow, and we question where is God, and will the sun ever shine again? Will this be the storm that destroys me?

However, I saw something once while on a plane flying over a storm that left me crying in my aisle seat and others around me avoiding eye contact. When you're above the storm, the sun is bouncing off the clouds and sending rainbows everywhere. It's beautiful. The people under the clouds, experiencing the storm couldn't see it, but the sun was still out and rainbows where everywhere.

It is not vital that I see the rainbow; it is nice when you can but not vital. What is important is that I know when I can't see Him, He sees me. He is watching, and He is keeping His covenant because the sun never stops shining; it just gets covered up by the storm.

When the disciples began to scream, Jesus spoke to them to calm them down by saying,

> *...But immediately He talked with them and said to them, "Be of good cheer! It is I; do not be afraid."*
> **(Mark 6:50)**

He did not yell at them or even scold them, He talked to them and note what He said. *"Be of good cheer!* This is almost funny they are scared to death from the storm, and His approach. Now He's saying, have some fun, laugh, rejoice. Paul makes this same request in Philippians 4:4 **Rejoice in the Lord always. Again I will say, rejoice!** The apostle uses the word always for a reason. He instructs from a Roman prison to a group of people suffering for their faith to rejoice. It seems that it is important to Jesus that His followers laugh, have a cheerful heart, even in stormy, scary circumstances.

He was not just letting them know it wasn't a ghost; He was assuring them that He was there, and they didn't have to be afraid. *"It is I"* was the Son of God assuring them that everything happening in their life at that moment was under His Sovereign Control. He was in the storm He was in its purpose, its timing, and its answer.

When Moses was afraid to go to Pharaoh in Egypt to speak for God and asked how he would explain his mission, God simply told Moses, "tell him I Am sent you." That is precisely what Jesus is telling His fearful disciples and us today. He is in the storm, He is in the timing, He is in control.

We will find peace only as we recognize He see's us and is control of every aspect of our storm. We don't have to understand the purpose, we don't have to understand when it will pass, we don't even have to understand the answer, but we must trust that He sent it; He controls it, and we may not understand but we can trust Him in the storm.

Peace and even joy can come in our storms when we trust not just what He can do but trust in who He is. He is a faithful, loving all powerful God that wants His children to have joy and cheer.

When God permits His children to go through the furnace,
He keeps His eye on the clock and His hand on the
thermostat. His loving heart knows how much and how long.
                                                    Warren Wiersbe

Chapter 8

The Ultimate Result of the Storm

Before we close out this section of the Mark chapter six storm we must look at verse 52 which sums up the story of this storm at sea. As a matter of fact it allows us to almost understand the storm. Why Jesus sent them into it, why He left them in it all night, and why He came to them scaring them to death in answer to their need.

> *"For they had not understood about the loaves,*
> *because their heart was hardened".*
>
> **(Mark 6:52)**

Note the end of verse 52, ***because their heart was hardened".*** Jesus sent this storm and all its confusion and turmoil because of the condition of their heart. Something they failed to understand about the loaves had put this whole storm scenario into their lives. Something about that feeding of the five thousand and how it played out revealed that their heart was hard and something had to be done to soften it. What was it?

You must look back and read Mark 6 verses 30 through 44 for signs of hard hearts.

Was it that although Jesus had been moved with compassion for the multitude the disciples really wanted to send them away, so they could begin their retreat?

They were excited when the miracle was performed and thousands were fed but, not because they had compassion for the hungry but loved the fact that it would promote their agenda. Many organizations and churches practice acts of generosity to the needy, but often it is not due to compassion for the needy. As a matter of fact, they would be greatly concerned if any of the needy they give food to wanted to be a part of their church or organization. They want the good publicity that comes along with giving to the needy. They want to claim the blessings that are promised to those that give to the needy. Their giving is not motivated by a compassion for the needy but by a self motivated promise to the generous.

As hurricane Isabel subsided in Edenton, my brother who had kept me abreast of its position, called again to let me know it was really over now and asked if we had suffered much damage. Looking out from our windows, I noticed tree limbs and pine needles all over the yard. A few window panes had been broken by flying debris, and some shingles had blown off the house, but it didn't look so bad. The peanut warehouse across the street had lost its roof, and part of it was in the yard, but it really was not too bad, from my window looking out.

Then my children and I decided to take a walk around the neighborhood behind our house where we regularly walk for exercise. So with my wife still sleeping, we ventured outside. What we saw then made me call my brother back and tell him I lied. Huge trees where down in the road and on houses and cars. In one place on the road I walk daily for exercise, the water level was chest high. Houses were flooded and many of the big waterfront homes in our community were simply washed out into the Albemarle Sound.

According to Wikipedia the results of Hurricane Isabel totaled 16 directly related deaths, over 6 million people were left without power, some for weeks, before it was restored. The estimated total damage to homes and property was over 3 billion US dollars. Storms always have results. Hurricane Isabel, though not as severe as storms like Katrina and others, changed the landscape of our little town forever. Homes that once were showplaces are now gone. Beautiful old water oaks that once lined Main

Street were gone as they simply left big craters in the ground where they were uprooted.

When storms come they always change things. God sends or at least allows the storms to come into our lives to change things. The things changed outwardly during our storms are what affect us the most, but these are not as big a concern of God as the things changed inwardly.

God is more concerned with the condition of our heart than with the comfort of our lives.

Storms come into our relationships and family not to destroy the relationships but to change our heart concerning the relationship.

Storms come into our lives physically to change our heart and teach us to rely on Him for strength to do His will. Paul learned this in praying three times for his "thorn in the flesh" to be removed and God responded that "His Grace was sufficient for you" God's strength is made perfect in our weakness.

Storms come into our finances to teach us to look to Him as our provider and to depend not on a career or a pay check but to depend on Him.

The biggest target of our storms, the thing that needs to be uprooted and changed is our heart. The prophet Jeremiah said this concerning the heart,

> *⁹ "The heart is deceitful above all things, And desperately wicked; Who can know it? ¹⁰ I, the Lord, search the heart, I test the mind, Even to give every man according to his ways, According to the fruit of his doings.*
> **(Jeremiah 17:9-10)**

We don't like to hear this concerning our hearts. We like to hear "follow your heart", "trust your heart" and "do what your heart tells you to do" but Jeremiah calls the heart deceitful, and then goes on to say that it will lie to you more than anything. The heart is wicked and will lead you astray. God will send a storm to search, and test your heart, and change it to what He desires it to be as we accept His ways.

It's interesting that verse 52 of Mark 6 says "**they had not understood**". I have been bringing out the hard to understand things in a storm this entire section. Maybe we are being told that instead of trying to understand the storms and what God is doing in the storms we should focus on trusting Him trying to understand the deceitful condition of our heart and how we need to yield it to God.

As we go through storms, there is always some well meaning Christian friend who will come along and quote **Romans 8:28.** *And we know that all things work together for good to those who love God, to those who are the called according to His purpose.*

When we hear this, we begin to rack our brains trying to figure out how this terrible storm is going to work out for our good. However, we must pay careful attention to that last phrase, *according to His purpose.*

The promise is not that it will work out our purpose but His purpose. What is His purpose? To understand this we must go to the next verse in Romans 8.

> *For whom He foreknew, He also predestined to be conformed to the image of His Son…*
>
> **(Romans 8:29)**

God's purpose is that we be conformed to the image of Christ. He will send things and do things in our lives to conform us like clay in the hand of the potter. The end result is that we be conformed into the image of His Son and our Lord.

Please take special note of this statement:

God is not as concerned with our comfort as He is in conforming us to His Son's image. We get the idea that God's job is to make us comfortable and meet all our wants. His purpose for us is that we may have the heart of compassion that His Son has and He will do what is necessary to create that new heart in us.

He will make us uncomfortable if that can be used to make us like Christ. The life of faith and fellowship with Christ is not about comfort but conforming.

In our next section we will see how when our hearts begin to rely on Him more, and we find our peace in Him, He will begin to do great things in our lives even in the midst of the storm. We will also look at ways to understand and examine our hearts during the storms of our lives.

Section II - Finding Peace in the Storm – Think it out

In the second section of the book we discuss finding peace in storms of life. What is brought out is that during a storm, whatever area it comes from, health, financial, relational or other. It is often difficult to figure out what God is doing and why He is doing it so severely. It get's hard to pray, hard to trust, yet real peace comes not from understanding what He is doing, but trusting Him.

Scriptural Reading: Proverbs 3:5-6 & Philippians 4:6-7

Trust in the Lord with all your heart, And lean not on your own understanding; ⁶ In all your ways acknowledge Him, And He shall direct your paths. **(Proverbs 3:5-6)**

Be anxious for nothing, but in everything by prayer and supplication, with thanksgiving, let your requests be made known to God; ⁷ and the peace of God, which surpasses all understanding, will guard your hearts and minds through Christ Jesus.
(Philippians 4:6-7)

Notice, the writer of the Proverb does not tell us to trust that the Lord will do exactly what we think He should do. It is not an instruction to trust what He will do, but to trust Him. Trust that He is all wise, all loving and all powerful. Then the writer goes on to warn us to lean not or trust not our own understanding. We think if we can understand what God is doing we can have peace. Peace comes as in "all" our ways as we simply acknowledge He is in it and His will, and His glory is what we seek.

Paul goes on in Philippians to instruct that the peace of God that can keep our hearts and minds at peace comes, not through understanding but through prayer (the worship of God for who He is), supplication (trusting God to supply what we really need in the storm) and thanksgiving (praise to God for all the blessings He has supplied for the storm). This peace can come as the storm rages and you and the people around you can't understand or explain how the peace is there but the circumstances are terrible.

44

Discussion Questions:

1. Is it possible that often part of our distress in the storms comes from trying to figure God out instead of trusting Him?

2. Does our prayer in the storm often involve more of telling Him how to fix it than worship and trust in His wisdom and grace during it?

3. Have you ever experienced an unexplainable peace during a traumatic event in your life?

If so, did this peace come from a complete understanding of what God was doing or from a complete trust in Him?

Section 3

Finding Power to Overcome the Storm

²⁷ But immediately Jesus spoke to them, saying, "Be of good cheer! It is I; do not be afraid."

²⁸ And Peter answered Him and said, "Lord, if it is You, command me to come to You on the water."

²⁹ So He said, "Come." And when Peter had come down out of the boat, he walked on the water to go to Jesus. ³⁰ But when he saw that the wind was boisterous, he was afraid; and beginning to sink he cried out, saying, "Lord, save me!"

³¹ And immediately Jesus stretched out His hand and caught him, and said to him, "O you of little faith, why did you doubt?" ³² And when they got into the boat, the wind ceased.

³³ Then those who were in the boat came and worshiped Him, saying, "Truly You are the Son of God."

Matthew 14:27-33

Playing in the Storm

As Isabel blew through our town, the estimated wind speed when hitting land was sustained gust, lasting one minute or longer, of 105 mph. I'm sure it had slowed down some by the time it got to Edenton, but it was still packing a wallop. To help you understand this effect, have you ever rolled down the window of your car while traveling say 65 or 70 mph on the interstate and stuck your hand out the window. The wind resistance if you try to push your palm against the wind is often too strong to maintain. Now imagine going 100 mph.

My children are made much like their father. While mom slept and the wind howled, we tried to find ways to spend our time. Remember the power had gone out early in the storm so TV, video-games and the computer were out. We played board games until that got boring and then we got adventurous.

First we challenged each other to step out on the front porch and try to remain standing against the wind for as long as we could. We are very competitive and stop watches are often used. I was winning this contest easily because I have a low center of gravity (I'm short) and I am a very level person (I have a bubble in the middle). I also outweighed my competition by well over 100lbs (I'm fat). As this competition heated up we gained courage in the storm.

Our house is on the main road that comes into town but because of the hurricane there was no traffic. Across the road from us is a road sign approximately 30 yards from our front door. The challenge was to see who could run out the front door, cross the front yard, cross the road, touch the road sign and get back without getting knocked down by the wind and rain with the best time. It was exhilarating. I did pretty good staying up against the wind, it was the running part that gave me problems. Did I mention I'm fat and not exactly physically fit?

That game gave us some sense of overcoming the storm. If we made it without falling, we had conquered the storm. Even if we fell, it still gave a sense of power over the storm.

In the storm we looked at in Mark chapter 6 something happened that Mark doesn't mention, but in Matthew's record of this same storm, he brings out something that happened that is remarkable.

Some believe, as do I, that much of Mark's gospel is based on things Peter told him about those years with Jesus. Maybe Mark doesn't mention what happened because Peter, in humility did not relay this because of his involvement. I am glad that Matthew chose to tell about Peter's special walk on the storm, for the lessons we can learn from it.

Chapter 9

Peter's Radical Request

As we discussed in the last chapter, finding peace in the storm comes when we gain assurance that Jesus is there watching us and with us. That He is carrying out a greater purpose with the storm and that we are being changed for His glory. As He assured these scared men in the boat of His presence and power watching over them in the storm, I am sure they all began to feel a calm and peace even though the storm was still raging around them. Then Peter did something that I believe left the others thinking that somewhere during this long night of fighting the storm, Peter had lost his mind.

> *But immediately Jesus spoke to them, saying, "Be of good cheer! It is I; do not be afraid." ²⁸ And Peter answered Him and said, "Lord, if it is You, command me to come to You on the water."*
>
> **(Matthew 14:27-28)**

Of all the characters and personalities in the Bible, Peter may be the one I relate to most. If you know anything about this fisherman/disciple you know he has some personality traits that are good but can also get him into trouble. He was bold enough to speak his mind, although sometimes it would have been better to remain quiet. He had leadership and tended to rise to the top, but sometimes he just wasn't sure where to lead once he had a following. He was sincere in his love and faith, just misappropriated his zeal and often made a fool of himself. I can relate.

This was one of those instances where I'm sure the other disciples thought, "there goes Peter again, spouting off one of his ideas." "Peter what are you thinking?" "Let Jesus rebuke the wind and sea again, calm things down, and let's get out of here." "OK, you're on your own here." But Peter was very serious; he wanted to do more than hunker down in this boat like he has all night.

Maybe Peter was one of those guys like me that gets a little stir crazy and is ready to get out of this boat he's been in all night. Maybe he was claustrophobic. Maybe like the Bishop's (other than my wife) Peter has a hard time just waiting for a storm to pass and wants an adventure. Whatever his reason and logic, Peter makes a very illogical request. ***"Lord, if it is You, command me to come to You on the water."***

As a pastor for the past 25 years, I have come to realize my "gifts". The things I'm good at and the things I'm not so good at, as a pastor. Pastors are called upon to wear a lot of hats and some I wear well; some not so well. One of the things I seem to do well is counseling. I guess I'm a good listener and the Holy Spirit moves on me to apply some scriptural principle that is applicable to the circumstance I am listening to, most of the time.

Often the situations that come to me are in a crisis. The fact that they have called the preacher and set up an appointment is an act of desperation most of the time. A piece of advice I often give is that during this time of crisis when your emotions are running wild, do not make any rash life changing decisions. Give it some time to settle down, and when you're thinking rationally, then make the decisions needed to help your circumstances. I think I have learned this from personal experience but maybe I haven't learned it that well, because I still make stupid decisions in storms.

If I had been Peter's counselor during this storm, I would have advised that he sit down, shut up, and give it some time. I'm glad I wasn't there, and I'm glad Peter would have ignored me. (As I suspect many of my counselees do)

If we look closer at Peter's request though, we realize he was not as irrational as he first appears.

"Lord, if it is You" Peter understood that only with Jesus could anything extraordinary be done. He would not have dared attempt this trick at home, without Christ but realized this storm would provide a unique opportunity to do something big with Christ. Maybe this statement implies that Peter had doubts about this being the Lord. But then again who else did he know that could have come walking to them on the sea. Maybe Peter remembers the power Jesus had given them to cast out demons and heal the sick and wanted to find out if this water walking power was also transferable.

"command me" Not promise me you'll fix this storm, but speak to me and call me out of the boat to do something during the storm. The others were satisfied with His presence being with them. They were quoting verses like, *"He'll never leave us nor forsake us"*, but Peter wanted to do something while in the storm. He wanted a command, new marching orders in the storm. What if we began to, instead of saying we're going to do something for Jesus as soon as this storm passes, asked Him to give us marching orders while the storm raged.

"to come to You" Peter wanted to get closer to Jesus. He was living with the motto, "I'd rather be with Jesus on the stormy water than without Him on the safe boat." If Jesus is in the boat Peter wanted to be in fellowship with Him. If He was out in the sea, Peter wanted to be out in the sea with Him.

"on the water." This was the kicker. He was asking to do all this, gain assurance, get a call, get closer to Jesus, by walking on water. He knew that he could not do this alone. As a fisherman he had been around water, in water, above water and under water but had never walked on the water. If this was to be done, it would be done in the power of Jesus not in his own power. This was something he would not be able to do even if the sun had been shining and the water was calm. He was asking to do it while the storm raged.

In defense of the, don't make rash decisions advice, Peter waited to hear from Christ before stepping out of the boat.

Most of the time, when we are faced with a storm in our life we think of all the things we hope to do if this storm ends. Sometimes we even bargain with, "God, if you will take care of this problem I will go to church more, tithe, go to the mission field etc… What if we were to dare to ask God to give us a new call on our lives if the storm doesn't end? What if we decided to play outside while the storm raged?

Is this so radical? Maybe? But is it possible that God has placed us in a storm to wake us up and get us to do the things we always thought about doing but were too busy to do when the sun was shining and we had other things on our mind. Tell that friend about Jesus while you're going through your own battles. Write that book, teach that class, make that step and open that door, while you're still being tossed by the storm.

Peter was obviously willing to take a risk, and people that do great things for God must be willing to take risk. It might be safer staying in the boat, you might fail if you take the risk, but then again you might just walk on water.

Chapter 10

Peters Risky Walk

If I may refer you back to my "remote replay" hopes in eternity this is a definite must scene. I love this story but so much is left to the imagination.

> *²⁹ So He said, "Come." And when Peter had come down out of the boat, he walked on the water to go to Jesus.*
> **(Matthew 14:29)**

Did Jesus shake his head and laugh thinking, "Peter only you" and then say "Come on" in an "Okay Peter come on but be careful" way, like a parent when their child insist they are ready to take the training wheels off.

Did Peter jump in with both feet or step very carefully? I would guess the latter with extreme caution.

What was the look on His face when he took his first step? What was the look on the faces of the guys that were still in the boat when Peter started water walking?

How far did he walk? Was it just a few steps or a few feet? You deeper theologians may find an answer in Revelation, but I want to think he went at least a few feet.

All these things are left for speculation, but one thing is told; Peter walked on water. Don't you know he reminded these guys of this when they questioned his ideas? We are told that there was a competition between James, John and Peter over places of authority beside Christ. I'm sure Peter reminded them often, "None of you have walked on water." At the last supper one of the reasons Jesus washed the disciple's feet is that none of them had offered to do so as they came in. Don't you know Peter was thinking or maybe even said it, "I'm not washing anybody's feet, I walked on water."

Maybe you've heard this expression used in a negative connotation concerning someone that is thinking too highly of themselves, "They think they can walk on water". Peter didn't just think it; he did it.

My diagnosis of Peter is that he was so loud and vocal at times speaking when he should have remained quiet to compensate for some deep seated insecurities. Not, that I have spent any time with Peter nor that I have any training to make a diagnosis, but I have watched a lot of television talk shows with psychologist. This event had to help with the insecurity. As a matter of fact, it may have made him even more obnoxious. It was the acme of his life he would never forget; he had walked on water.

> *³⁰ But when he saw that the wind was boisterous,*
> *he was afraid; and beginning to sink he*
> *cried out, saying, "Lord, save me!"*
>
> **(Matthew 16:30)**

However, I'm sure when he got too boastful about it, the other guys would quiet him down by reminding him what happened next. He began to sink. He failed. I've failed enough to know there will always be someone around to remind you. Usually it's someone that never walked on water themselves. As a matter of fact, in my experience, I have a hard time believing one of those guys hunkering down in the boat didn't start telling him what a crazy idea this was even before he stepped over the edge of the boat. They probably shook their heads and thought to themselves, "well

I don't want to pop his bubble, but this is not going to work." "I hope he isn't too disappointed when he falls on his face." But remember, in spite of his failure, Peter walked on water. In a storm, in a terrible situation, after a terrible night of struggling to survive, he did it.

People are made differently and respond to storms differently. My daughter has two children a boy and a girl. The greatest thing a child can give their parents is grandchildren. The grandchildren call me Boo-Boo. They respond to storms differently. If my granddaughter hears thunder, she begins to cry and wants someone to hold her. My grandson however hears thunder and yell's "Boo-Boo, let's go outside and watch the lightning."

Some folks are satisfied with hunkering down in the boat and waiting for Jesus to show up and calm the storm; others see the storm as an opportunity to go out in the storm and watch the lightning.

Often an emphasis is placed on failure. Peter did begin to sink, and I'm sure was reminded of this. But we never come to the place of overcoming our storms if we don't face the risk of being overcome by the storm. I think Matthew recorded this event to bring out one important fact about going through storms with Jesus. He can empower us to do great things in our storms, and He will be with us to save us if and when we fail.

This lesson is what made Peter preach during the stormy days after the crucifixion and resurrection of Christ. It's what made Peter a leader of the early church and motivated him to boldly preach the gospel to a very hostile audience in Jerusalem. Not that he had done something great by walking on the water. But that Christ could do great things with loud mouth, confused, not so disciplined disciples if they trusted Him.

Peter not only learned about being able to do great things in the power of Christ, but he also learned something about failure.

> ³¹ *And immediately Jesus stretched out His hand and caught him, and said to him, "O you of little faith, why did you doubt?"*
>
> **(Matthew 14:31)**

When we fail, and we all do, Jesus is faithfully there to catch us. He will not let us fall. Did Jesus whisper in Peter's ears the words of gentle rebuke, ***"O you of little faith, why did you doubt?"***

Does He still do this to us? Gently reminding us that He is more powerful than our storm, and if we will keep our eyes on Him, He can do more that catch us when we fall. He can empower us to succeed.

Chapter 11

The Progressive Growth

In Chapter 5 we mentioned the popular quote from the prophet Isaiah concerning waiting upon the Lord and discussed that God's waiting room was difficult always especially in the storms. However the greatest growth comes as we look to Him while waiting for the storms to cease. We are more in tune, more hungry to hear from Him and see Him move while in the waiting room. Isaiah speaks of a process of strength while waiting on the Lord.

> *³¹ But those who wait on the Lord Shall renew their strength;*
> *They shall mount up with wings like eagles, They shall*
> *run and not be weary, They shall walk and not faint.*
> **(Isaiah 40:31)**

I don't think Isaiah is speaking about what will happen to you after the storm has passed and after God has answered, but while in the waiting room. The prophet is giving instructions of what to do while you wait, and the renewed strength you will gain while waiting.

The prophet is instructing Israel, while waiting on God to deliver, to find the strength to soar like eagles, and if you get too tired to fly then run, and if you get too tired to run then walk, but don't faint. Don't stop, some of the greatest things you will ever do for God, some of the highest points you will ever soar, will not be when the skies are clear, but when the cloud cover is heavy and all is dark around you.

Instead of hunkering in the boat and hiding in the storm, Peter walked on water, but I want us to notice that the other disciples did some growing of their own that fearful morning.

> *³² And when they got into the boat, the wind ceased. ³³ Then those who were in the boat came and worshiped Him, saying, "Truly You are the Son of God."*
> **(Mark 14:32-33)**

Go back with me to the first storm in Mark 6, and note the exclamation that the disciples that were in fellowship with Jesus made after He rebuked the wind and sea, and everything calmed down. ***"Who can this be, that even the wind and the sea obey Him!"*** The King James Version said ***"What matter of man is this that even the wind and sea obey Him."*** The disciples that day came to the realization in that first storm at sea, that Jesus was no ordinary man.

Now note their exclamation of worship after the storm that had left them all struggling all night, the ghostly appearance of Christ walking on water, and the power of Christ in allowing Peter to take a short walk. When the wind ceased, they worshipped Him. This is big. Jews worship one God, Jehovah and are very careful not to attribute any worship to anything or anyone but God. They worshipped Christ and made this exclamation, ***"Truly You are the Son of God."***

They had grown in their understanding that Jesus was more than an extraordinary man; He was the Son of God and worthy of worship.

Remember the game we played as children "Simon Says." One child would stand and offer commands to the other children lined up in front of him. Whoever followed the commands precisely and got to Simon first would win. The catch was, you had to obey the command only with the preface of "Simon Says." If a command was made without the "Simon

Says" before it, and you did it, you had to go back to the start. Commands like "take two baby steps" or "take one giant step" had to have the preface "Simon Says" before it.

Without question "Simon" won the game that night on the sea. Simon Peter asked Jesus to command him to take steps to Him, and Jesus commanded, and Simon walked. However the others on the boat made some steps of their own. They stepped from seeing Jesus as a mere extraordinary man, which He was, to seeing Him as the Son of God, the man that was also deity.

In Matthew 16 Jesus asked His disciples the most important question of following Him,

> *13 **When Jesus came into the region of Caesarea Philippi, He asked His disciples, saying, "Who do men say that I, the Son of Man, am?"***
>
> **(Matthew 16:13)**

Their reply was what He expected;

> *14 **So they said, "Some say John the Baptist, some Elijah, and others Jeremiah or one of the prophets." 15 He said to them, "But who do you say that I am?" Simon Peter answered and said, "You are the Christ, the Son of the living God."***
>
> **(Matthew 16:14)**

Of course, Peter got to answer this question for them because he had won the game that night on the sea, but all of them agreed this was the Christ, the Son of the living God, and they had grown to believe this most important truth of who Jesus was by growing in the storm.

This growth came through their obedience to His command when they were made to get in the boat and go to the other side. It may have been a somewhat reluctant obedience. Their hearts may not even have been in the right place which is often the case as we enter our storms, but they were following Jesus and growing in the knowledge of who they were and most importantly, who He was and what they could become with Him.

The point is we don't get to pick when the storms will come; we don't get to pick how long they'll last, and we don't get to choose the answer that will eventually calm our storm. What we can do, is choose to look to the Master of the Sea and find hope in him. We can also get risky like Peter and learn some things He can do through us in the storm.

Section III – Finding Power to Overcome the Storm

In Section three we discussed Peter's amazing walk on the stormy sea. We looked at our tendency to "hunker down in the boat" during the storms of our lives but need to consider that God may be using the storm to call us out into a more daring walk with Him.

Scriptural Reading: II Corinthians 12:7-10

> *[7] And lest I should be exalted above measure by the abundance of the revelations, a thorn in the flesh was given to me, a messenger of Satan to buffet me, lest I be exalted above measure. [8] Concerning this thing I pleaded with the Lord three times that it might depart from me. [9] And He said to me, "My grace is sufficient for you, for My strength is made perfect in weakness." Therefore most gladly I will rather boast in my infirmities, that the power of Christ may rest upon me. [10] Therefore I take pleasure in infirmities, in reproaches, in needs, in persecutions, in distresses, for Christ's sake. For when I am weak, then I am strong.*
>
> *God had done many powerful things in Paul's life and due to his calling as the apostle to the Gentiles had given Paul amazing revelations of truth. To keep the apostle humble, he had also been given a "thorn in the flesh." You might call this Paul's long lasting personal storm.*

1. Paul says this "thorn in the flesh" was given to him, who gave him this special gift?

2. Paul calls this "thorn in the flesh" a "messenger of Satan to buffet him" was Satan the giver or the deliverer of this gift?

3. Paul tried to return this special gift three times but was denied, with instruction from God on the benefit of the gift. Have you ever pleaded with God to fix your storm and been denied?

4. Paul began to "boast" and "take pleasure" in his infirmities and found the grace and power to do things in the strength of God. Can we overcome our storms and walk on them like Peter did when we realize God's "grace is sufficient"? Have you ever walked on your storm and did amazing things to God's glory in the midst of suffering?

Section 4

Finding our Priorities in the Storm

27 And when it was decided that we should sail to Italy, they delivered Paul and some other prisoners to one named Julius, a centurion of the Augustan Regiment. 2 So, entering a ship of Adramyttium, we put to sea, meaning to sail along the coasts of Asia. Aristarchus, a Macedonian of Thessalonica, was with us. 3 And the next day we landed at Sidon. And Julius treated Paul kindly and gave him liberty to go to his friends and receive care. 4 When we had put to sea from there, we sailed under the shelter of Cyprus, because the winds were contrary. 5 And when we had sailed over the sea which is off Cilicia and Pamphylia, we came to Myra, a city of Lycia. 6 There the centurion found an Alexandrian ship sailing to Italy, and he put us on board.

7 When we had sailed slowly many days, and arrived with difficulty off Cnidus, the wind not permitting us to proceed, we sailed under the shelter of Crete off Salmone. 8 Passing it with difficulty, we came to a place called Fair Havens, near the city of Lasea.

9 Now when much time had been spent, and sailing was now dangerous because the Fast was already over, Paul advised them, 10 saying, "Men, I perceive that this voyage will end with *disaster and much loss, not only of the cargo and ship, but also our lives." * ¹¹ *Nevertheless the centurion was more persuaded by the helmsman and the owner of the ship than by the things spoken by Paul.* ¹² *And because the harbor was not suitable to winter in, the majority advised to set sail from there also, if by any means they could reach Phoenix, a harbor of Crete opening toward the southwest and northwest, and winter there.*

¹³ *When the south wind blew softly, supposing that they had obtained their desire, putting out to sea, they sailed close by Crete.* ¹⁴ *But not long after, a tempestuous head wind arose, called Euroclydon.* ¹⁵ *So when the ship was caught, and could not head into the wind, we let her drive.* ¹⁶ *And running under the shelter of an island called Clauda, we secured the skiff with difficulty.* ¹⁷ *When they had taken it on board, they used cables to undergird the ship; and fearing lest they should run aground on the Syrtis Sands, they struck sail and so were driven.* ¹⁸ *And because we were exceedingly tempest-tossed, the next day they lightened the ship.* ¹⁹ *On the third day we threw the ship's tackle overboard with our own hands.* ²⁰ *Now when neither sun nor stars appeared for many days, and no small tempest beat on us, all hope that we would be saved was finally given up.*

²¹ *But after long abstinence from food, then Paul stood in the midst of them and said, "Men, you should have listened to me, and not have sailed from Crete and incurred this disaster and loss.* ²² *And now I urge you to take heart, for there will be no loss of life among you, but only of the ship.* ²³ *For there stood by me this night an angel of the God to whom I belong and whom I serve,* ²⁴ *saying, Do not be afraid, Paul; you must be brought before Caesar; and indeed God has granted you all those who sail with you.* ²⁵ *Therefore take*

heart, men, for I believe God that it will be just as it was told me. ²⁶ However, we must run aground on a certain island."

²⁷ Now when the fourteenth night had come, as we were driven up and down in the Adriatic Sea, about midnight the sailors sensed that they were drawing near some land. ²⁸ And they took soundings and found it to be twenty fathoms; and when they had gone a little farther, they took soundings again and found it to be fifteen fathoms. ²⁹ Then, fearing lest we should run aground on the rocks, they dropped four anchors from the stern, and prayed for day to come. ³⁰ And as the sailors were seeking to escape from the ship, when they had let down the skiff into the sea, under pretense of putting out anchors from the prow, ³¹ Paul said to the centurion and the soldiers, "Unless these men stay in the ship, you cannot be saved." ³² Then the soldiers cut away the ropes of the skiff and let it fall off.

³³ And as day was about to dawn, Paul implored them all to take food, saying, "Today is the fourteenth day you have waited and continued without food, and eaten nothing. ³⁴ Therefore I urge you to take nourishment, for this is for your survival, since not a hair will fall from the head of any of you." ³⁵ And when he had said these things, he took bread and gave thanks to God in the presence of them all; and when he had broken it he began to eat. ³⁶ Then they were all encouraged, and also took food themselves. ³⁷ And in all we were two hundred and seventy-six persons on the ship. ³⁸ So when they had eaten enough, they lightened the ship and threw out the wheat into the sea.

³⁹ When it was day, they did not recognize the land; but they observed a bay with a beach, onto which they planned to run the ship if possible. ⁴⁰ And they let go the anchors and left them in the sea, meanwhile loosing the rudder ropes; and they hoisted the mainsail to the wind and made for shore. ⁴¹ But striking a place where two seas met, they ran the ship

*aground; and the prow stuck fast and remained immovable,
but the stern was being broken up by the violence of the waves.*

*[42] And the soldiers' plan was to kill the prisoners, lest
any of them should swim away and escape. [43] But the
centurion, wanting to save Paul, kept them from their
purpose, and commanded that those who could swim
should jump overboard first and get to land, [44] and
the rest, some on boards and some on parts of the ship.
And so it was that they all escaped safely to land.*

Acts 27:1-44

The Loss to the Storm

The estimated loss in dollars from hurricane Isabel in Eastern North Carolina was close to half a billion dollars. There was only one death directly related to the hurricane in our county. My personal realization of loss in the storm came from a few isolated instances.

Just a few days before Isabel hit, I was in my insurance company's office and the line was unbelievable. One of the things I love about living in a small town is simply the lines aren't as long. You can get the tags renewed on your car or even renew your driver's license without setting aside a whole day to wait in line at the DMV. However, this day I stood in an unbelievable long line at my insurance company. When I asked why so many people were there that day I understood.

Our county is a farming community. Peanuts, cotton, and other crops give livelihood to many of the people in Chowan County. My insurance company specializes in insuring farmers. The line was farmers insuring the crops that were in the ground because if this hurricane came like they said it was going to, their crops would be wiped out and their income from the hard work and expense of seeding and preparation would be lost. I learned that day that storms can cause loss in areas I didn't even realize.

A few hours after Isabel had passed my boys of course were walking through neighborhoods exploring the damage. They came home and told me that Cindy, a single mom that lived in the next neighborhood over, wanted me to come over and look at her car. A tree had blown over on her car, and she was wondering if it was totaled.

I walked with the boys over to Cindy's, and when I rounded the corner and could see her driveway, I began to laugh. The tree was huge and had fallen directly down the center of the car from front to back. The car was flattened like a pancake with all four tires flattened and the wheels broken off at the axel just poking out. She asked very concerned, "Do you think they'll total it preacher?" When I quit laughing, I assured her they would not try to fix that vehicle. I have seen cars in the scrap yard after being crushed in better shape than hers.

The town of Edenton has a beautiful waterfront with many beautiful homes lining its shores. One home in particular that my wife and I had often admired had recently been purchased by some good friends of ours, Marshall and Teri Wiliford. We decided the day after the hurricane to walk down to the waterfront and check on the Wilifords to see how they had made out. The roads were impassable so you had to walk and it was a little over a mile from our house. The walk downtown was amazing as we saw the devastation of our beautiful historic town. As we got closer to the Wiliford home we could see some activity and people going in and out of the front door. I mentioned to my wife that although I could see they had lost the boat dock and Gazebo that was built over the water, it appeared from the front of the house that it was OK. We knocked on the door, and Marshal invited us in with a grin on his face. As we walked in, we realized the Wiliford's view of the water had improved. Hurricane Isabel had taken the back half of their home away, the kitchen, the back porch and the back wall were somewhere in the Albemarle Sound. The beautiful waterfront home was eventually demolished.

When we left the Wilifords destroyed home to walk back, we watched a man living on the waterfront go out to his driveway to a shiny brand new Ford Thunderbird and open the door for, what became obvious, was the first time since the storm. When he opened the door, water came pouring out of the car. He told me he had just bought it two weeks earlier.

Later that day a sheriff's deputy that is a member of our church and good friend invited my wife and me to ride with him in his patrol car to the section of our county that was hit the hardest. This neighborhood has a mixture of homes and mobile homes on nicely wooded lots, all just off the Albemarle Sound. It was like a war zone with many homes and property destroyed by the trees that had once made their lots so nice. Then he showed us a nice mobile home with a tree that had fallen directly across it. The girl that lived there had gone out to her car to leave, and another tree came across the car and took the life of this young lady.

Witnessing the loss people experienced was the hardest part of dealing with the storm. But there is no question the loss of the young lady that died in the storm was the greatest for the family and friends that knew and loved her.

Storms have a way of making us reevaluate the things in our life. What are the things that really matter? What are the things that if the storm destroys it, we can live without? What are the things that cannot be replaced by insurance and FEMA? Storms have a way of making us readjust our list of priorities.

When the storm hits, our priorities change quickly. As I mentioned before in the first section, little boat people quickly decide they want in the boat with Jesus when the storm hits.

I want us to go to a storm at sea story that is recorded in the book of Acts and learn about priority adjustments in the storm.

Chapter 12

The Danger of Calm Seas

The apostle Paul had been arrested in Jerusalem by the Jewish leaders who hated him. They hated Jesus and crucified Him. Now they especially hated Paul because he had been one of them and had been converted on the Damascus Road and had become a follower of this one Jesus whom they had crucified. They wanted to execute Paul, but he being a Roman citizen had made an appeal to appear before Caesar. They had no choice but to honor his request.

Paul is placed under arrest and handed over to the Roman commander. After avoiding a conspiracy by the Jews to kill him before he gets to Rome, Paul appears before Felix the Roman governor and Agrippa the King or tetrarch of the Palestinian region appointed by the Roman senate. Felix and Agrippa agree to send Paul to Rome to appear before Caesar.

And when it was decided that we should sail to Italy, they delivered Paul and some other prisoners to one named Julius, a centurion of the Augustan Regiment. ² So, entering a ship of Adramyttium, we put to sea, meaning to sail along the coasts of Asia. Aristarchus, a Macedonian of

Thessalonica, was with us. ³ And the next day we landed at Sidon. And Julius treated Paul kindly and gave him liberty to go to his friends and receive care. ⁴ When we had put to sea from there, we sailed under the shelter of Cyprus, because the winds were contrary. ⁵ And when we had sailed over the sea which is off Cilicia and Pamphylia, we came to Myra, a city of Lycia. ⁶ There the centurion found an Alexandrian ship sailing to Italy, and he put us on board.

(Acts 27:1-6)

Paul is handed over to a Roman guard named Julius in charge of delivering prisoners to Rome. Chapter 27 of Acts is about this voyage of prisoners, Roman guards and sailors to Rome. The arrangements have been made aboard a ship in Myra headed to Italy that was also carrying cargo to be sold in Rome. Because of the season Paul advises the men to wait until winter passes to make the journey. They ignore his advice because the wind is blowing softly and the sea is calm.

⁷ When we had sailed slowly many days, and arrived with difficulty off Cnidus, the wind not permitting us to proceed, we sailed under the shelter of Crete off Salmone. ⁸ Passing it with difficulty, we came to a place called Fair Havens, near the city of Lasea.

⁹ Now when much time had been spent, and sailing was now dangerous because the Fast was already over, Paul advised them, ¹⁰ saying, "Men, I perceive that this voyage will end with disaster and much loss, not only of the cargo and ship, but also our lives." ¹¹ Nevertheless the centurion was more persuaded by the helmsman and the owner of the ship than by the things spoken by Paul. ¹² And because the harbor was not suitable to winter in, the majority advised to set sail from there also, if by any means they could reach Phoenix, a harbor of Crete opening toward the southwest and northwest, and winter there.

(Acts 27:7-12)

Life gets complicated. Often the complications come in calm weather. When the weather is great, we live as if it always will be that way and add more things. Calm seas have a way of putting us to sleep with the false sense of security that as nice as things are going, there's no way things could go bad.

When finances are good, we buy more often on credit with the assurance that we will be able to pay the bill. Then a financial storm hits. Lay-offs, job losses, cut-backs, health issues and we realize that things have to change. We begin to realize we had lost focus of what really mattered and things we thought we had to have become a burden. Storms have a way of changing the things we thought were important.

When the relationships with the people we love are sailing along smoothly, we tend to neglect taking the necessary steps to build the relationship. We neglect our spouses, our children, our parents and take an attitude that says this is my time to take care of me and do what I want to do. Then enters infidelity, rebellion, disagreements and the relationship begins to sink. We start rethinking how we spent our time and who we spent it with.

When we are in relatively good health and we haven't had to call the doctor for a while we start being careless in our diet and exercise. Then we start having pain or sickness and the health storm involves lots of doctors, prescriptions, and regrets. If we had exercised more, ate less or at least more healthy.

We make the same mistakes with our spiritual life. We neglect church, prayer and time with God because we feel we have it all under control. The things of God really are not very high on our priority list simply because with the way life is going I don't have time. We still love God and make efforts to show spiritual concern, but life's demands crowd Him out.

> *¹³ When the south wind blew softly, supposing that they had obtained their desire, putting out to sea, they sailed close by Crete. ¹⁴ But not long after, a tempestuous head wind arose, called Euroclydon.*
>
> **(Acts 27:13)**

The phrase, ***that they had obtained their desire,*** mixed with the soft blowing south wind, became a great deceptive factor in the decision of these men. Great desire and seemingly favorable circumstances does not necessarily dictate the will of God. Often when our heart greatly desires something, and it seems like things are working outwardly in favor of us achieving that desired thing, we mistake it as God's will. As mentioned earlier the heart can be very deceptive, also favorable circumstances like south winds can deceive us into making what later becomes a dreadful decision.

I am really not sure when the most dangerous seasons of our lives are. Is it when we are in a storm and desperately seeking God and His presence or is it when we are sailing on smooth seas and neglecting the things that really matter. Calm seas have a way of lulling us to sleep, while storms tend to wake us up and make us sensitive to the things that are important in our lives.

David's infamous sin with Bathsheba and her husband happened when David had reached a place in his life of victory as a king, and he did not go out to battle.

> *¹¹ It happened in the spring of the year, at the time when kings go out to battle, that David sent Joab and his servants with him, and all Israel; and they destroyed the people of Ammon and besieged Rabbah. But David remained at Jerusalem.*

> *² Then it happened one evening that David arose from his bed and walked on the roof of the king's house. And from the roof he saw a woman bathing, and the woman was very beautiful to behold. ³ So David sent and inquired about the woman. And someone said, "Is this not Bathsheba, the daughter of Eliam, the wife of Uriah the Hittite?" ⁴ Then David sent messengers, and took her; and she came to him, and he lay with her, for she was cleansed from her impurity; and she returned to her house. ⁵ And the woman conceived; so she sent and told David, and said, "I am with child."*
> **(II Samuel 11:1-5)**

Often our biggest failures happen not when we are hungry, but when we are full.

Ignoring Paul's advice and setting sail in the open sea, the sailors and guards aboard that ship found out all too quickly regardless of how calm the sea seemed yesterday, storms do come.

Chapter 13

Losing Control to the Storm

Everyone loves to feel that they are in control of their lives. Volumes of books are written on determining your destination and choosing your own destiny. We hear about choosing the right path that leads to success, and of course the practical side of that is correct. We do need to have vision and determine a destination, but the storm factor can take that all away.

The owner of the ship that Paul was on had determined where they were going and how they were going to get there. He had determination and experience with sailing and felt sure they would make their destination. He probably had an ETA estimated time of arrival. Had it turned out the way he planned, he would have been rewarded for his early arrival, his taking the risk and it paying off. He would have given speeches attributing his success to experience and determination.

The fact is they didn't make it. They had not planned for the storm. Instead of being in control of his destiny, he had surrendered control to the storm.

> *So when the ship was caught, and could not*
> *head into the wind, we let her drive.*

(Acts 27:15)

When storms hit, we find that it becomes hard to *"head into the wind"* even if that is the direction we need to go. We find that we have no control of where we will end up or if this storm might just be the end of us. This may be the scariest thing about storms is we find ourselves totally at the mercy of the storm and have no choice but to *"let her drive."*

Truth is none of us really has as much control as we like to think. Storms make us realize this. We like to think we are in control of our finances, our family and the other factors in our lives. Then events come that knock us off course with the possibility that things may never turn out the way we dreamed they would. I doubt there is anyone forty or over reading this book that would say your life is exactly on the course you dreamed and planned for when you were twenty or twenty-five.

Your relationships and family are probably not exactly what you planned. Your children haven't become exactly what you dreamed. Your finances and career are not on the course you set when you were young. Your health is not what you thought it would be. The people you thought would always be there in your life have died or the relationship got lost on a stormy sea. Storms come and change the dynamics of our life, and we realize we hadn't planned for it, nor could we control it.

What I want us to see from the Acts 27 storm is that the men on the ship with Paul did what they could do, but then it was left to the storm to drive them. Note some of the things they could do.

> **And running under the shelter of an island called Clauda, we secured the skiff with difficulty.**
>
> **(Acts 27:16)**

The larger ships in that day would tow a small boat behind them for setting anchor off shore and taking passengers to land. This small boat was called a skiff. The thought behind securing the skiff was that if the larger boat began to sink, they could possibly be saved using the smaller skiff. They understood you should have a plan B for backup.

> **17 When they had taken it on board, they used cables to undergird the ship;**
>
> **(Acts 27:17)**

Large ropes were thrown over the sides of the boat with men diving under the boat and bringing the ropes under to the other side and then tied around to literally wrap the ship up to keep it from coming apart.

> *...and fearing lest they should run aground on the Syrtis Sands, they struck sail and so were driven.*

There is a term we like to use in describing people that love to micro manage everything and everybody around them; "Control Freaks." As you read this you are thinking of someone in your life, a parent, a boss, a sibling or friend at work or at church. Those people that feel it is their calling to intrude on the decisions and choices of the people around them.

Maybe that's what these sailors thought of Paul when he at first cautioned them about sailing the open sea in this season. They wanted to be in control of their own destinies. I think all of us have a little control freak in us. We exercise it over our children, our church, or our jobs, but all of us at some time, have had to come to the place where we had to let go, and letting go, and letting the wind of circumstances drive us, may be the hardest choice of our lives.

As the storm rages it is important that we face the fact that we can't control some of the things that are happening and may happen. But there are things we can do and must do. During the storms we must bring the things we have neglected back to a place of importance in our lives. We must secure our relationships, and the things that matter, undergird and hold closely to the things we can't lose while accepting some things will be lost.

The Well Known Serenity Prayer Says

> *God grant me the serenity*
> *to accept the things I cannot change;*
> *courage to change the things I can;*
> *and wisdom to know the difference.*

Chapter 14

Losing Dreams in the Storm

¹⁸ And because we were exceedingly tempest-tossed, the next day they lightened the ship. ¹⁹ On the third day we threw the ship's tackle overboard with our own hands. ²⁰ Now when neither sun nor stars appeared for many days, and no small tempest beat on us, all hope that we would be saved was finally given up.

(Acts 27:18-20)

As the sailors on this ship laden with cargo and prisoners headed to Rome looked over the ship, before the storm, I'm sure they envisioned a good pay day. They were already going with the cargo and now that Julian the centurion, assigned to deliver the prisoners to Rome, had struck a deal with the captain of the ship this meant a bonus on their pay. There was probably an extra bonus thrown in if they were to make deliveries early. That and the fact that it would be much nicer to spend the winter in Pheonix or possibly Rome, the hub of the world at that time, than some port called Fair Haven. Along with the calm sea giving them dreams of a good year they were elated. Then the storm hit, and dreams began to unravel.

We tend to make plans, dream dreams, and forge forward when things are going well. However, often the storms of life cause the dreams to slip away along with the lack of sleep. Hope is lost and we face what some call reality.

Dreamers are important; without dreamers much of the technology we enjoy today would never have come. Dreams can be just the reality of tomorrow, so dreaming is not necessarily unrealistic. However, when storm clouds blow in and begin to erode our hopes, sometimes we face the reality that the plans we made were apparently not God's plans.

James 4:13-16 is one of those dream killer passages of the Bible that particularly apply to our text:

> *¹³ Come now, you who say, "Today or tomorrow we will go to such and such a city, spend a year there, buy and sell, and make a profit"; ¹⁴ whereas you do not know what will happen tomorrow. For what is your life? It is even a vapor that appears for a little time and then vanishes away. ¹⁵ Instead you ought to say, "If the Lord wills, we shall live and do this or that."*

James warns of the sin of presumption and boasting about our plans and how we will make them happen. We like to think we are writing the book of our lives, but ultimately God is the author. Our disappointments and depression over the storms come when God brings in a sudden plot change that we had not anticipated.

Have you ever been in a grocery store or department store when things were going on sale? Years ago this was done with a hand held "pricing gun", and they marked things down. Some stores would close the store the day before the sale, and employees would work all day marking the new sale prices on the items in the store. Storms have a way of causing price changes in our lives.

Before the storm the cargo and the tackle on the ship Paul was sailing on were of the greatest value, and the skiff and ropes were priced low. Now we see them tossing cargo and tackle overboard with their own hands, a sign of a major mark down in value. Skiffs and ropes that had been on the discount aisle, were now of high value, and their price went way up.

When Hurricane Isabel hit Eastern North Carolina, there were many reports of "price gouging." People came into town with electric generators that normally sold for $400.00 to $500.00 and were selling them out of the back of trucks for $1000.00 to $1200.00. Tree removal services and stump grinders were making a fortune for their services. Even gas stations that could find a way to get electricity to operate their pumps increased their prices on gas, and it had nothing to do with the government and gas shortages. They could raise the price due to the law of supply and demand. Fresh drinking water and ice, things you normally take for granted, became hot commodities.

The storms of life have a way of doing this also. Marriages, family and health are some of things we don't put much time or energy into when things are going smoothly, but these things become much more valuable when the storms hit. Recreation, fancy cars and homes, boats and hobbies that seem to take so much of our time and energy and fill our dreams become the things we don't even think about and can't believe we spent so much time on when the storm comes. We are willing to toss all the things that consumed our time, energy and money overboard just to get out of our storm alive.

In I Timothy, Paul wrote to Timothy the young pastor about contentment:

> **6 Now godliness with contentment is great gain. 7 For we brought nothing into this world, and it is certain we can carry nothing out. 8 And having food and clothing, with these we shall be content. 9 But those who desire to be rich fall into temptation and a snare, and into many foolish and harmful lusts which drown men in destruction and perdition. 10 For the love of money is a root of all kinds of evil, for which some have strayed from the faith in their greediness, and pierced themselves through with many sorrows.**
>
> **(I Timothy 6:6)**

I don't know how it was in Timothy and Paul's day, but in our day, dreaming about better things is encouraged and pushed. Commercials on television are designed to make us fantasize about that new car, or "Lifestyle's of the Rich and Famous" make us fantasize about a bigger house, with more gadgets and electronics. Americans especially, live to get more and more and then have yard sales to get rid of all we have accumulated. We love that new thing for about a month, and then see one that is nicer and begin to dream again. Instead of thankfulness for all we have and contentment, we desire more.

Then when a storm hits our dreams change. Instead of thinking so much about a newer car or home we just fantasize about that marriage working out, or that child coming back home, or having the money to pay for the house or car we currently have. Storms rearrange our dreams.

These sailors quit dreaming about partying in a nice port, or getting a good paycheck for the goods they were delivering, and started fantasizing about surviving this storm.

Our dreams sometime serve as ways to escape, and we place great value on our dreams. Some dreams are unrealistic, and some are reachable. However, the thing that must have greatest value is not our dreams but God's plan and purpose for our lives that are for His glory. If His pleasure and bringing a smile to His face becomes our priority, then we can face the storm accepting that even when it was not in our plan, it presents a way to bring glory to Him.

That is why in the midst of hopelessness and despair Paul was able to shine brightly for God and bring Him glory while the storm raged.

Chapter 15

Finding Hope in the Storm

Acts 27:21-44

There are over one million suicides reported every year in our world with ten to twenty million attempted suicides each year. There are various reasons people give for attempting to end their lives. Drug addiction, poverty, depression, failure and others are given as the cause. I am not a psychiatrist, but I think the root cause of suicide is simply hopelessness. Whatever the situation, if it's drugs and the hopelessness of breaking the addiction, relational and the hopelessness of things working out or even financial and the hopelessness of ever getting ahead, it can lead to wanting out.

In our region after Hurricane Isabel, the mental health business picked up. People fought depression looking at the magnitude of the loss and felt any attempt at restoring the damage was hopeless. In areas like New Orleans when Hurricane Katrina devastated their lives, the suicide rate over doubled in the next months for that region.

Storms can lead to hopelessness because of the loss. When we come to realize we are really not in control, and our dreams for the future are never going to come true. That life isn't Disney Land and even if we "wish upon a star", some dreams aren't going to happen; it can lead to hopelessness.

When hope is given up, then the natural attempts at self-preservation die. Then the next step down is self-destruction.

> *...all hope that we would be saved was finally given up.²¹ But after long abstinence from food,*
>
> **(Acts 27:20-21)**

The men on board the ship with Paul reached a place where all hope was lost. They went days without food because "what's the use in eating if you're going to die." Then as you reach the end of the chapter, you find a plot by the sailors to abandon the prisoners and their guards and head out on the skiffs. Self preservation has kicked back in. They must have found some hope somewhere.

> *...then Paul stood in the midst of them and said, "Men, you should have listened to me, and not have sailed from Crete and incurred this disaster and loss. ²² And now I urge you to take heart, for there will be no loss of life among you, but only of the ship. ²³ For there stood by me this night an angel of the God to whom I belong and whom I serve, ²⁴ saying, Do not be afraid, Paul; you must be brought before Caesar; and indeed God has granted you all those who sail with you. ²⁵ Therefore take heart, men, for I believe God that it will be just as it was told me...*
>
> **(Acts 27:21-25)**

The hope came from an old preacher that had heard from God and encouraged them to take heart. We too can find hope in desperate situations as we take the time to hear from God when hopelessness is noisily blowing our lives apart.

They had ignored the man of God's advice earlier about the threat of a storm and set sail when the wind and seas were calm. Paul had to take this opportunity to say "I told you so" and he does. That was more than a chance to say "I told you so" but a chance to get them to listen now. He was the wise one in the crowd that had been forced into this storm by their dreams and plans. Now he had their ear. More importantly he had given God his ear and heard a message from an angel of His God.

Paul's hope was not in his future plans to sit in a Roman prison and appeal to Caesar. If anyone had a right to lose hope and not care what happened to them, it was Paul. He was a prisoner planning to speak to the Roman Emperor about his faith in Jesus. More than likely he would be sentenced to death anyway.

Paul's hope was in the fact that he belonged to the God of this storm and His God had a plan for him. God had assured Paul he would in fact speak to Caesar, and no storm could thwart this plan. He was also assured that each of the men on the ship with him would also be spared.

Hope comes when we come to realize we belong to God, and He has a plan for us regardless and maybe through some of the things going on around us. Hope comes when we are listening for His voice and not the voices around us screaming that it's hopeless. Hope comes when we align ourselves with people that know Him and hear his voice and begin to listen to them.

> *...Therefore I urge you to take nourishment, for this is for your survival, since not a hair will fall from the head of any of you." *[35]* And when he had said these things, he took bread and gave thanks to God in the presence of them all; and when he had broken it he began to eat. *[36]* Then they were all encouraged, and also took food themselves. *[37]* And in all we were two hundred and seventy-six persons on the ship. *[38]* So when they had eaten enough, they lightened the ship and threw out the wheat into the sea.*
> **(Acts 27:34-38)**

Paul encouraged and restored hope in the men aboard this ship during the storm. They ate; they were encouraged. We don't know how many if any of these men became believers in Paul's God, but everyone on that ship wanted what Paul was saying to be true and joined him as he gave thanks over the meal. I like to believe some of them called on the name of His Lord that day on the ship.

Think for a moment, these men who ignored this guy who seemed a little weird as they began this journey are now saying grace with him and eating and listening to him talk about his God. Would this have been possible had there not been a storm?

When times are darkest, light is most needed. When the storms are raging, the opportunity to represent the God of the storm is best. We tend to avoid storms, hate storms, but storms and how we deal with them may be greatly used by God

> *...And so it was that they all escaped safely to land...*
> **(Acts 27:44)**

The cargo and stuff they would use to make profit couldn't give hope. The plans of time in Rome with money, couldn't give hope. Only the God of an old apostle could give them hope. Which of these things should be on top of our priority list?

When the storms hit, and they will, what should be our priority and what can we afford to toss overboard to find hope? There will be loss, but the thing we must have is hope.

Section IV – Finding our Priorities in the Storm

Section four of the book went to the story of Paul's shipwreck at sea on the way to Rome. We discussed the sailors on the ship with Paul that began to refocus what was valuable and what was expendable as the storm raged. Storms have a way of changing our dreams, our plans, and the things that matter the most to us.

Scriptural Reading: Matthew 6:31-34

> [31] *"Therefore do not worry, saying, What shall we eat? or What shall we drink? or What shall we wear? [32] For after all these things the Gentiles seek. For your heavenly Father knows that you need all these things. [33] But seek first the kingdom of God and His righteousness, and all these things shall be added to you. [34] Therefore do not worry about tomorrow, for tomorrow will worry about its own things. Sufficient for the day is its own trouble.*

So much of what occupies our minds has not happened and there is a good possibility will never happen.

1. What has occupied your thought life today? What have you planned for tomorrow?
2. How do you determine what is a priority in your life?
3. When you face a storm what changes in your plans and thoughts?
4. Where is your relationship with Christ on your priority list? Look at your calendar, your check book and your clock to answer this question.

Section V

Facing Personal Responsibility in the Storm

Now the word of the Lord came to Jonah the son of Amittai, saying, ² *"Arise, go to Nineveh, that great city, and cry out against it; for their wickedness has come up before Me."* ³ *But Jonah arose to flee to Tarshish from the presence of the Lord. He went down to Joppa, and found a ship going to Tarshish; so he paid the fare, and went down into it, to go with them to Tarshish from the presence of the Lord.*

⁴ *But the Lord sent out a great wind on the sea, and there was a mighty tempest on the sea, so that the ship was about to be broken up.*

⁵ *Then the mariners were afraid; and every man cried out to his god, and threw the cargo that was in the ship into the*

sea, to lighten the load. But Jonah had gone down into the lowest parts of the ship, had lain down, and was fast asleep.

⁶ So the captain came to him, and said to him, "What do you mean, sleeper? Arise, call on your God; perhaps your God will consider us, so that we may not perish."

⁷ And they said to one another, "Come, let us cast lots, that we may know for whose cause this trouble has come upon us." So they cast lots, and the lot fell on Jonah. ⁸ Then they said to him, "Please tell us! For whose cause is this trouble upon us? What is your occupation? And where do you come from? What is your country? And of what people are you?"

⁹ So he said to them, "I am a Hebrew; and I fear the Lord, the God of heaven, who made the sea and the dry land."

¹⁰ Then the men were exceedingly afraid, and said to him, "Why have you done this?" For the men knew that he fled from the presence of the Lord, because he had told them. ¹¹ Then they said to him, "What shall we do to you that the sea may be calm for us?"- for the sea was growing more tempestuous.

¹² And he said to them, "Pick me up and throw me into the sea; then the sea will become calm for you. For I know that this great tempest is because of me."

¹³ Nevertheless the men rowed hard to return to land, but they could not, for the sea continued to grow more tempestuous against them. ¹⁴ Therefore they cried out to the Lord and said, "We pray, O Lord, please do not let us perish for this man's life, and do not charge us with innocent blood; for You, O Lord, have done as it pleased You." ¹⁵ So they picked up Jonah and threw him into the sea, and the sea ceased from its raging. *¹⁶ Then the men feared the Lord exceedingly, and offered a sacrifice to the Lord and took vows.*

¹⁷ Now the Lord had prepared a great fish to swallow Jonah. And Jonah was in the belly of the fish three days and three nights

Jonah 1 & 2

Responsibility

Just two weeks before Hurricane Isabel came by our house, before I had ever heard about her, I had become concerned about a pine tree in my yard. It was tall, skinny, ugly and was only about ten yards from my house. If it ever blew over, it would surely come right through my kitchen. I talked to some guys about taking it down, and they came to look it over.

I was most concerned about how they would do it. If it fell to the west it would come through my house. If it fell to the east it would block the road. If it fell north it would damage some trees I wanted to keep. There was a very little space to the south that it could probably safely fall if they could get it in that narrow margin of yard.

Those guys knew what they were doing. They used a bucket truck to go as high as they could and began to cut the top out of the old pine. Then they continued to cut five foot sections from the top until they reached the trunk which they cut off as close to the ground as possible. They hauled off sections of the tree, and in one day it was gone. The next week I had someone grind out the stump that was left, and it was over.

Two weeks later the hurricane came through and without a doubt based upon the direction of the wind had I not taken responsibility for that old pine, my kitchen would have had a natural made skylight that leaks.

Although I am sure God protected my family and my home, had I not exercised some responsibility in removing the tree, the storm would have done great damage to my home.

We must accept the fact that often the storms that rage into our lives are of our own making. Irresponsible life styles and decisions lead us into situations that can destroy our lives. The greatest responsibility of a believer is obedience. Regardless of our feelings and desires, we must surrender to the will of our Lord.

Chapter 16

The Disobedient Prophet

Throughout my ministry God has allowed me to preach to and minister to teenagers in various ways. I served as a Youth Pastor at my home church; I have served in Youth Camp Ministries as director or speaker every year for 30 years. I have lead in Youth Retreats and preached Youth Revivals throughout my ministry. People have often told me I had a way of connecting with young people. I only know I love being around them and ministering to them.

Inevitably the most asked question I get from young people is how can I find the Will of God for my life. My answer is not one they seem to like. I simply tell them that you find God's will for your future by walking in what you know to be God's will day by day. One of my clichés that I'm sure I got somewhere else is: "You will stumble across God's will for your future as you walk in the path of God's will daily."

I do believe our creator has a plan for our lives individually, call it God's perfect will for our lives. The God who designed us, designed us for a particular life.

God's will is not simply obedience, but I connect it with passages in Ephesians chapter one that speak of "the good pleasure of His will."

³ Blessed be the God and Father of our Lord Jesus Christ, who has blessed us with every spiritual blessing in the heavenly places in Christ, ⁴ just as He chose us in Him before the foundation of the world, that we should be holy and without blame before Him in love, ⁵ having predestined us to adoption as sons by Jesus Christ to Himself, <u>according to the good pleasure of His will,</u> ⁶ to the praise of the glory of His grace, by which He made us accepted in the Beloved. (Ephesians 1:3-6)

having made known to us the mystery of His will, according to His good pleasure which He purposed in Himself.

(Ephesians 1:9)

In Him also we have obtained an inheritance, being predestined according to the purpose of Him who works all things according to the counsel of His will,

(Ephesians 1:11)

I like to describe it as living to bring a smile to God's face. Not just obeying His laws but pleasing Him with our choices and decisions.

God has a plan for us, but we do not necessarily have to live out that plan. He has given us choices called a "free will." If you envision God's will as a set point we get to decide how close to that point or how far away from that point we will live.

I don't believe His will is a mystery to be found. I think as we get to know Him, we basically know what pleases Him and what doesn't. We just have to decide if we want to live today pleasing Him or pleasing ourselves. Is it important to us if He is smiling or just that we are happy?

Not that He wants us miserable because I believe the greatest joy is found in living within the plan of the one who created us. This joy is there in the storms and the sunshine. If we have chosen to reject His plan and live for our own desires, the circumstances can change our joy. The writer of Hebrews speaking of Moses says that he was *"choosing rather to suffer affliction with the people of God than to enjoy the passing pleasures of sin."* Moses chose to suffer with the people of God because he came to realize what God's will and plan was for his life. Walking outside of God's plan may have served to bring passing pleasure, but walking within the will of God brought lasting joy.

It is amazing to me that the God of the universe has a plan for my life and is willing to reveal His plan to me as I walk with Him.

In our text God has come to a prophet named Jonah and revealed to him His plan. Up until this time Jonah had been a very successful prophet. According to II Kings, God had used Jonah to deliver a message to King Jeroboam II about reclaiming land that had previously been in the hands of the enemy and the King had heeded his message and brought victory to Israel.

> *He restored the territory of Israel from the entrance*
> *of Hamath to the Sea of the Arabah, according to*
> *the word of the Lord God of Israel, which He had*
> *spoken through His servant Jonah the son of Amittai,*
> *the prophet who was from Gath Hepher.*
>
> **(II Kings 14:25)**

I'm sure this had made a national hero out of Jonah and he had a comfortable life being taken care of by the King out of appreciation. Then God had a new assignment that Jonah balked at.

> *Now the word of the Lord came to Jonah the son of Amittai,*
> *saying, ² "Arise, go to Nineveh, that great city, and cry out*
> *against it; for their wickedness has come up before Me."*
> *³ But Jonah arose to flee to Tarshish from the presence of*
> *the Lord. He went down to Joppa, and found a ship going*
> *to Tarshish; so he paid the fare, and went down into it, to*
> *go with them to Tarshish from the presence of the Lord.*
>
> **(Jonah 1:1-3)**

God commissioned Jonah to go to Nineveh and preach, so that they might be spared from God's judgment and wrath. This didn't sit very well with Jonah, and he decided to run.

I'm not sure what made this prophet of God, this man that God had spoken to directly, choose to run from God. Maybe it was prejudice or pride. I'm not sure what makes me often flinch at what I know in my heart God desires, but I think it is connected with our desires verses God's desire.

Nineveh was a gentile city that was infamous for its sin and debauchery. It was a definite enemy of Jonah's beloved country, and he was a patriot. Jonah probably felt toward Nineveh the way many Americans felt toward Bagdad after 9/11. Jonah had possibly been praying that God would judge Nineveh, and now God was telling Him to go preach to them that they might be saved from judgment.

I'm sure Jonah's prejudices, the way he was raised, the political environment he was in all cried out in opposition to what God was asking him to do. So Jonah ran.

We often do the same thing. There are times when our history, our personal agendas, and our pride go against the things we know God desires in our lives, and we run or attempt to run from the presence of God.

The greatest responsibility of the people of God is to know the will of God and do it. Often we claim we don't know God's will, but in fact we do as the point of decision faces us. We want to claim ignorance, but we know if we are choosing to bring a smile to the Father's face or simply please ourselves.

Paul speaking to the church at Ephesus instructed them:

> *¹⁷ Therefore do not be unwise, but understand*
> *what the will of the Lord is.*
>
> **(Ephesians 4:17)**

Paul would not instruct us to know what the will of the Lord is, if it were something we could not know. God provides His will and the wisdom to know what His will is, we often just choose to ignore it.

Failure to please Him is the act of irresponsible behavior that can often lead to raging seas in our lives.

Chapter 17

The Providence of God

Often as believers we find great comfort in the thought from Paul's letter to the church at Philippi.

> *And my God shall supply all your need according to His riches in glory by Christ Jesus.*
>
> **(Philippians 4:19)**

The belief in the providential care of our Heavenly Father for his children should bring us great comfort in the time of need. However, have you ever considered the not so pleasant side of His providence? God will supply our need even if we don't think we need it or don't want it.

If we need it, He will supply direction even if we don't like His directions and are comfortable in our own plans. If we need bread, God supplies bread,; if we need strength, God provides strength; and we love the hope this thought brings. But if we need a whipping, God provides a whipping. Jonah learned a lot about the providence of God.

Notice in Jonah chapter 1 the things God provided for the prophet.

When Jonah needed a new assignment according to verse 1, God came to Him and gave him guidance. God told him to go the Nineveh and preach. God provided direction:

> *Now the word of the Lord came to Jonah the son of Amittai, saying, ² "Arise, go to Nineveh, that great city, and cry out against it; for their wickedness has come up before Me."*
> **(Jonah 1:1)**

Jonah rejected this assignment and got on a ship headed the other way, so Jonah needed correction. According to verse 4, God sent a storm. God provided this in order to give Jonah the correction and discipline he needed in his life. This is the kind of thing that we wish God would not provide.

> *But the Lord sent out a great wind on the sea, and there was a mighty tempest on the sea, so that the ship was about to be broken up...*
> **(Jonah 1:4)**

When you were a child, your parents at some time said before spanking you, "this is going to hurt me more than it hurts you" and then they proceeded to thrash you with a belt. I know this is politically incorrect today, but when mine did it to me, I have now come to realize I needed the whipping more than they wanted to whip me. My parents probably didn't supply this discipline nearly as much as I needed it.

God will supply the needed discipline when we need it every time, and often it comes in the shape of a storm. It tosses our life around; it changes our heart; and is used to bring us back to the place of God's plan for us that we chose to ignore.

The writer of the book of Hebrews reminds us of God's faithfulness in providing chastisement when we need it.

> *⁵ And you have forgotten the exhortation which speaks to you as to sons: "My son, do not despise the chastening of the Lord, Nor be discouraged when you*

are rebuked by Him; ⁶ For whom the Lord loves He
chastens, and scourges every son whom He receives."

⁷ If you endure chastening, God deals with you as with
sons; for what son is there whom a father does not
chasten? ⁸ But if you are without chastening, of which
all have become partakers, then you are illegitimate and
not sons. ⁹ Furthermore, we have had human fathers
who corrected us, and we paid them respect. Shall we
not much more readily be in subjection to the Father
of spirits and live? ¹⁰ For they indeed for a few days
chastened us as seemed best to them, but He for our profit,
that we may be partakers of His holiness. ¹¹ Now no
chastening seems to be joyful for the present, but painful;
nevertheless, afterward it yields the peaceable fruit of
righteousness to those who have been trained by it.

(Hebrews 12:5-11)

The truth is that we are not always the victim of some random storm. The people around us like the sailors on the ship with Jonah were victims, but we are the reason for the storm. The storm is not sent to destroy us but to correct us. God's discipline or chastisement is not sent to cause us to faint but to get our attention, correct us and bring us into His plan for our lives. That we might experience the lasting joy and "peaceable fruit of righteousness" spoken of in the Hebrew passage.

The great thing about God's providence is that even when He sends a terrible storm to correct us, just before it destroys us, He sends along a life preserver. In Jonah's case the life preserver didn't seem too great, but it got Jonah back to where he was intended to be by His creator.

… So they picked up Jonah and threw him into
the sea, and the sea ceased from its raging…

(Jonah 1:15)

...Now the Lord had prepared a great fish to swallow Jonah. And Jonah was in the belly of the fish three days and three nights.

(Jonah 1:17)

A few days in the bellow of this large, living life raft and Jonah learned what God's perfect will was for his life. God provides what we need, when we need it, even if it smells a little fishy.

Chapter 18

The Fish Belly Prayers

Possibly one of the hardest disciplines of the Christian life is maintaining a regular prayer life. As I have mentioned in the earlier chapters of this book when you're in a storm, it gets easier to pray with passion for deliverance from the storm; but when the seas are calm, it's harder to maintain that regular communication with the Father.

But the hardest prayers to pray are what I will call the Fish Belly Prayers. These are the times when the storm is raging in your life and you know it's your fault. You ignored God's word, avoided His advice and made your own bad choices that have brought you to this place of despair. The "reap what you sew" principle has kicked in. You have sewn to the wind you are reaping the whirlwind. Now, knowing it's your fault that you're in this mess, how can you ask God for help? Surely you feel His reply is, "You got yourself in this mess, get yourself out." Thankfully God doesn't work that way. He is a God of grace and mercy and is waiting for us to call on Him.

Jonah is at this place in his life. He has disobeyed God's call and attempted to run from God's presence. Which as we all know is impossible because of God's omnipresence, although we still try. Jonah has reaped the whirlwind and now finds himself in a fish's belly which has saved him from dying but is not much more secure than the storm itself. As a matter of fact, the thing keeping him from perishing in the storm smells a little fishy.

> **Then Jonah prayed to the Lord his God from the fish's belly.**
> **(Jonah 2:1)**

God does hear our prayers in the storms of our own making, but I'd just like to notice three special acknowledgments that need to be made in fish belly prayers.

First I want to point out that Jonah acknowledged his personal responsibility to the people in his life that were caught up in his storm.

> **Then the men were exceedingly afraid, and said to him, "Why have you done this?" For the men knew that he fled from the presence of the Lord, because he had told them. ¹¹ Then they said to him, "What shall we do to you that the sea may be calm for us?"- for the sea was growing more tempestuous.**
>
> **¹² And he said to them, "Pick me up and throw me into the sea; then the sea will become calm for you. For I know that this great tempest is because of me."**
> **(Jonah 1:10-12)**

Whether we are willing to admit it or not our storms affect others around us. The people in our lives, our parents, our children, our friends and even our associates are affected when our irresponsible decisions bring dark clouds into our lives. An English poet named John Donne said it best in his 1624 prose, "No man is an Island." Our lives are intricately connected, and our storms affect those connected to us.

Jonah had tried to run from God and country and become a self made man answering to no one. He learned that we always need others. He needed sailors to get him away from Israel, Nineveh and God. He built this relationship by simply keeping his spiritual condition to himself. But eventually it caught up to him, and the storm was not just his but the people onboard that ship with him.

> *But Jonah had gone down into the lowest parts of the ship, had lain down, and was fast asleep.*
>
> *⁶ So the captain came to him, and said to him, "What do you mean, sleeper? Arise, call on your God; perhaps your God will consider us, so that we may not perish."*
>
> **(Jonah 1:5-6)**

It is interesting that the person bringing on the storm is at first, the one that is least affected by the storm. While the sailors were battling and confused where the storm came from, Jonah was sleeping. Sometimes storms are sent to wake us up and make us face responsibility for our actions.

The captain challenged Jonah to call on his God, and Jonah somewhere during this discourse admitted that his God was the one that was sending this storm, and he was running from Him. He didn't want to call on God; he was trying to get away from Him.

> *¹² And he said to them, "Pick me up and throw me into the sea; then the sea will become calm for you. For I know that this great tempest is because of me."*
>
> **(Jonah 1:17)**

At this point Jonah reached the place of hopelessness I wrote about in the previous section of this book. He didn't want to obey God's call; he could not escape God's presence, and now his disobedience was putting others in danger. The best thing he could do is die. If he were dead, they would be safe; he wouldn't have to go to Nineveh, and it would be over. Jonah's advice to the sailors, was throw me to the storm. They didn't want to, but for survival they plead for mercy from Jonah's God and tossed him over. Their storm ended, but little did they know that God wasn't through with Jonah.

*13 Nevertheless the men rowed hard to return to land,
but they could not, for the sea continued to grow more
tempestuous against them. 14 Therefore they cried out
to the Lord and said, "We pray, O Lord, please do
not let us perish for this man's life, and do not charge
us with innocent blood; for You, O Lord, have done
as it pleased You." 15 So they picked up Jonah and
threw him into the sea, and the sea ceased from its
raging. 16 Then the men feared the Lord exceedingly,
and offered a sacrifice to the Lord and took vows.*
(Jonah 1:13-16)

After acknowledging his responsibility for the storm from the fish's belly Jonah made another acknowledgment that I feel is essential, Jonah acknowledged God's grace and mercy in hearing his prayer and also acknowledged God faithful discipline in judging his sin.

*"I cried out to the Lord because of my
affliction, And He answered me.*

"Out of the belly of Sheol I cried, And You heard my voice.

3 For You cast me into the deep, Into the heart of the seas,

*And the floods surrounded me; All Your
billows and Your waves passed over me.*

*4 Then I said, I have been cast out of Your sight; Yet
I will look again toward Your holy temple.*
(Jonah 2:1-3)

I have heard preachers cry out against using God like a spare tire. Carrying God around to help us when a tire goes flat in our lives, then pulling Him out through prayer to help us is a common practice among believers. I agree that we should develop a prayer life before the storm comes and emphasized that in the first section of this book on "Preparing for the Storm". However, I think it is important that we realize that our relationship with God is not based on our faithfulness but His unconditional love for us. He wants us to call on Him, and although He would love a daily fellowship with us, He is in His mercy waiting for our call. He sends the storm not to destroy us but to bring us to a fish belly so that we will call on Him.

Jonah cried in his affliction and God heard. He acknowledged that God, not the sailors, had cast him into this stormy sea, and that God heard him in his despair. Although he had been "cast out of Your sight" to "look again toward Your holy temple" was a privilege provided by a merciful God.

Note the far reaching distance prayer can reach even when we have attempted to flee from God's presence.

> *I went down to the moorings of the mountains; The*
> *earth with its bars closed behind me forever;*
>
> *Yet You have brought up my life from*
> *the pit, O Lord, my God.*
>
> *⁷ "When my soul fainted within me, I remembered the Lord;*
>
> *And my prayer went up to You, Into Your holy temple.*
> **(Jonah 2:6-7)**

From the lowest pit in the depths of the ocean of despair, Jonah remembered the Lord. His cry went out from this low place and went up to God, to the heights of His holy temple. God hears our cries even from our deepest sinful pits.

Prayer even fish belly prayer will reach the ear of a merciful God as we begin to take responsibility for the storms He has sent to wake us up and get our attention.

The third acknowledgement Jonah made in this prayer after acknowledging responsibility and God's grace to hear is the acknowledgement that God and God alone has the power to save us from our desperate situation.

Jonah 2:9 contains one of my favorite all time phrases in the Bible; "*Salvation is of the Lord.*"

Jonah had come to a place that he realized if he was going to be delivered from this storm and fish belly situation, it would not be from running from the presence of God but from running to God. God and God alone could save him now. He could not save himself; he could do nothing but rely on God's sovereignty over this great fish to be delivered. God sent it all, and only God could change it.

We will never get to the place of complete obedience until we accept this truth, "*Salvation is of the Lord.*"

Upon acceptance of God's sovereign control over the situation, Jonah repented of his past choices and made new vows.

> *But I will sacrifice to You With the voice of thanksgiving; I will pay what I have vowed.*
>
> **(Jonah 2:9)**

Jonah had faced up to the responsibility of the storm, and God's mercy and power, and his responsibility to obey what God had called him to do.

Chapter 19

The Fish Puke Prophet

So the Lord spoke to the fish, and it vomited Jonah onto dry land.

(Jonah 2:10)

Earlier in this book I spoke of my "remote reruns in eternity thoughts". If there is a remote in heaven and we get to see instant replays of biblical events, I would like to see this one, as a big fish comes to shore and spits out Jonah on shore. Were there people at the beach that witnessed this? I know there are instances of fish washing ashore and getting stuck on sand bars, but this is the only instance I have heard of a man coming ashore from the fish.

What did Jonah look like? Had the fish's stomach acids bleached him white? Did he stink? Most vomit does stink and look nasty.

What we do know is that when God told Jonah to go to Nineveh and cry out against it this time Jonah didn't waste any time getting there. As a matter of fact, it may have been one of the most successful evangelistic campaigns of all time.

It took three days to walk through Nineveh. Jonah walked through the city during those three days, and his sermon was less than homiletic genius. He simply preached; *"Yet forty days, and Nineveh shall be overthrown!"* I'm not sure he even did it with much passion, but it was effective.

> *³ So Jonah arose and went to Nineveh, according to the word of the Lord. Now Nineveh was an exceedingly great city, a three-day journey in extent. ⁴ And Jonah began to enter the city on the first day's walk. Then he cried out and said, "Yet forty days, and Nineveh shall be overthrown!"*
>
> **(Jonah 3:3-4)**

Nineveh experienced revival. It even got to the king, and he repented. It was the kind of result any evangelist would love to put in his next newsletter.

> *So the people of Nineveh believed God, proclaimed a fast, and put on sackcloth, from the greatest to the least of them. ⁶ Then word came to the king of Nineveh; and he arose from his throne and laid aside his robe, covered himself with sackcloth and sat in ashes. ⁷ And he caused it to be proclaimed and published throughout Nineveh*
>
> **(Jonah 3:5-7)**

Jonah had followed God's will and preached and brought a smile to God's face to the point that God spared Nineveh.

> *Then God saw their works, that they turned from their evil way; and God relented from the disaster that He had said He would bring upon them, and He did not do it.*
>
> **(Jonah 3:10)**

However we find in chapter 4 of the book of Jonah that he was not so pleased.

But it displeased Jonah exceedingly, and he became angry. ² So he prayed to the Lord, and said, "Ah, Lord, was not this what I said when I was still in my country? Therefore I fled previously to Tarshish; for I know that You are a gracious and merciful God, slow to anger and abundant in lovingkindness, One who relents from doing harm. ³ Therefore now, O Lord, please take my life from me, for it is better for me to die than to live!"

(Jonah 4:1-2)

Jonah didn't report his successful evangelistic campaign; he didn't rejoice over these sinners that had come to repentance; in fact he filed a complaint with God. He acknowledges that he was well aware of the nature and heart of God, *for I know that You are a gracious and merciful God, slow to anger and abundant in loving kindness.* Yet he is showing that even though obedient to the call of God, he is not really concerned with the will of God.

The storm was passed; the sun was shining; he had been delivered by the providential hand of God. Yet he had no joy. As a matter of fact, he was deeply depressed to the point of wanting to die.

Joy in the storm or after it passes comes when our hearts have come to the place of desiring what God desires and rejoicing in what makes God rejoice. God reminds Jonah through an illustration with a plant that He cares for people.

Peter in his second epistle speaking of the coming judgment of God, and its delay reminds us;

The Lord is not slack concerning His promise, as some count slackness, but is longsuffering toward us, not willing that any should perish but that all should come to repentance.

(II Peter 3:9)

God's desires must become our desires; Gods love for His creature must be spread in our hearts so that come storm or sunshine, God's glory becomes our desire. From storm or sunshine joy comes not from the circumstances we find ourselves in, but from finding ourselves pleasing God.

Section V – Facing Personal Responsibility in the Storm

In this section we looked at Jonah the runaway prophet and noted that sometimes the storms are sent into our lives to get our attention and obedience to God's call on our lives. Not always but often the storms are our fault and others around us are affected.

Scriptural Reading: Hebrews 12:5-11

⁵ And you have forgotten the exhortation which speaks to you as to sons:

"My son, do not despise the chastening of the Lord, Nor be discouraged when you are rebuked by Him; ⁶ For whom the Lord loves He chastens, And scourges every son whom He receives."

⁷ If you endure chastening, God deals with you as with sons; for what son is there whom a father does not chasten? ⁸ But if you are without chastening, of which all have become partakers, then you are illegitimate and not sons. ⁹ Furthermore, we have had human fathers who corrected us, and we paid them respect. Shall we not much more readily be in subjection to the Father of spirits and live? ¹⁰ For they indeed for a few days chastened us as seemed best to them, but He for our profit, that we may be partakers of His holiness. ¹¹ Now no chastening seems to be joyful for the present, but painful; nevertheless, afterward it yields the peaceable fruit of righteousness to those who have been trained by it.

God loves His children, just the way we are, but He loves us too much to leave us that way. If we insist on exercising our will against His will for our lives, He will do what is necessary to bring us into the plan He has for our lives.

1. According to Hebrews 12:5 what are the two responses to God's chastening hand?
2. Have you ever doubted if you were God's child? Is chastening a way to find security?
3. How did you respond to your parents when they disciplined you? How do you respond to God's chastening?
4. When was the last time God had to give you a whipping?

Section 6

Recovering from the Storm

¹⁵ Then God spoke to Noah, saying, ¹⁶ "Go out of the ark, you and your wife, and your sons and your sons' wives with you. ¹⁷ Bring out with you every living thing of all flesh that is with you: birds and cattle and every creeping thing that creeps on the earth, so that they may abound on the earth, and be fruitful and multiply on the earth." ¹⁸ So Noah went out, and his sons and his wife and his sons' wives with him. ¹⁹ Every animal, every creeping thing, every bird, and whatever creeps on the earth, according to their families, went out of the ark.

²⁰ Then Noah built an altar to the Lord, and took of every clean animal and of every clean bird, and offered burnt offerings on the altar. ²¹ And the Lord smelled a soothing aroma. Then the Lord said in His heart, "I will never again curse the ground for man's sake, although the imagination of man's heart is evil from his youth; nor will I again destroy every living thing as I have done.

²² "While the earth remains, Seedtime and harvest, Cold and heat, Winter and summer, And day and night Shall not cease."

9 So God blessed Noah and his sons, and said to them: "Be fruitful and multiply, and fill the earth. ² And the fear of you and the dread of you shall be on every beast of the earth, on every bird of the air, on all that move on the earth, and on all the fish of the sea. They are given into your hand. ³ Every moving thing that lives shall be food for you. I have given you all things, even as the green herbs. ⁴ But you shall not eat flesh with its life, that is, its blood. ⁵ Surely for your lifeblood I will demand a reckoning; from the hand of every beast I will require it, and from the hand of man. From the hand of every man's brother I will require the life of man.

⁶ "Whoever sheds man's blood, By man his blood shall be shed; For in the image of God He made man. ⁷ And as for you, be fruitful and multiply; Bring forth abundantly in the earth And multiply in it."

⁸ Then God spoke to Noah and to his sons with him, saying: ⁹ "And as for Me, behold, I establish My covenant with you and with your descendants after you, ¹⁰ and with every living creature that is with you: the birds, the cattle, and every beast of the earth with you, of all that go out of the ark, every beast of the earth. ¹¹ Thus I establish My covenant with you: Never again shall all flesh be cut off by the waters of the flood; never again shall there be a flood to destroy the earth."

¹² And God said: "This is the sign of the covenant which I make between Me and you, and every living creature that is with you, for perpetual generations: ¹³ I set My rainbow in the cloud, and it shall be for the sign of the covenant between Me and the earth. ¹⁴ It shall be, when I bring a cloud over the earth, that the rainbow shall be seen in the cloud; ¹⁵ and I will remember My covenant which is between Me and you and every living creature of all flesh; the waters shall never again become a flood to destroy all flesh. ¹⁶ The rainbow shall be in the cloud, and I will look on it to remember the everlasting covenant between God and every living creature of all flesh that is on the earth." ¹⁷ And God said to Noah, "This is the sign of the covenant which I have established between Me and all flesh that is on the earth."

(Genesis 8:15-9:17)

Storm Recovery

Without question the most extensive effort related to Hurricane Isabel in eastern North Carolina in our region were the efforts to restore our little town back to normal. With the realization that things would never be the same as they were before it hit, we worked together to make it livable again.

The large old trees that were over a hundred years old and fell would be missed by the folks familiar with them, but for newcomers they would never know what it had looked like before. The stately homes that had been damaged beyond repair would be torn down and replaced by newer homes on the lots that were left. Much work has been done on the Edenton waterfront that has actually made it nicer for those evening walks my wife and I like to take. Life has been put back to normal, whatever normal is, and Isabel is a memory that we refer to in conversations about the big one that hit home.

Storms inevitably change things and change can be good or bad depending on the efforts we make in recovering from them.

I was amazed as the traffic started pouring into our town to help in recovery. Utility company trucks from all over came through town like a parade. These crews worked around the clock to replace power poles and power lines and restore power to the hundreds of homes without. Volunteers from everywhere came with chain saws and other tools to help and give aid to our devastated region.

I stayed in town after I sent my family to the mountains and worked in the relief efforts. I was assigned a group of Amish Men with chainsaws. These guys were amazing. I would drive them to find homes with trees fallen on the roof. I would ask permission of the owner of the home to take the trees off. Then I would let these guys go to work. They would take off climbing on roofs and tree limbs and in no time would have cut big trees up and cover the roof with tarps.

I was most impressed by the unity and cooperation of the town and volunteer workers. People working together for free around the clock to restore the things lost in the storm. We had to use discernment in these efforts to distinguish what we called the Needy from the Greedy. Some folks simply wanted to get something for free or make a profit from others loss. But the large majority simply wanted to help recover what was lost.

One of my fondest memories in the aftermath of the hurricane was on Sunday morning two days after Isabel had hit. Of course there was still no power or water anywhere in town and getting around in cars was impossible and still being discouraged by town authorities. The little church where I served as pastor was meeting in a small fitness center building we had bought and converted into a church building. It was in the neighborhood behind my house. There was no way to communicate about services that morning, so those of us who lived nearby just agreed to meet for a time of prayer and fellowship. No lights and no air conditioning meant leaving the doors open to try to let in enough light to see each other.

A musician and song writer that attended our church brought his guitar, and we had church. He had written a song that weekend about our town and its pain at the moment. I don't remember the words to that song, but I remember the overwhelming emotional moment we all shared as his song encouraged us that God was there for us as we recovered. That morning the sun was shining literally and in our hearts.

Chapter 20

The Ultimate Storm

Everyone has storm stories. Often people come to me for pastoral counseling and are not looking for any advice from me but simply want to tell someone about their storm. Sometimes it bothers me when they seem to feel theirs is worse than anyone else. Fact is everyone has gone through pain, heartache and scary times and at the time you're going through it, your situation consumes you.

Here in Genesis is the record of the greatest storm ever and the Noah family that went through it. I'm sure most of you are familiar with this storm. Apparently it was not just the forty days of rain which was bad enough but the "fountains of the deep" opened up as well and violently destroyed everything, everything on earth.

Now the flood was on the earth forty days. The waters increased and lifted up the ark, and it rose high above the earth. [18] The waters prevailed and greatly increased on the earth, and the ark moved about on the surface of the waters. [19] And the waters prevailed exceedingly on the earth, and all the high hills under the whole heaven were covered. 20 The waters prevailed fifteen cubits upward, and the mountains were covered. 21 And all flesh died that moved on the earth: birds and cattle and beasts and every creeping thing that creeps on the earth, and every man. 22 All in whose nostrils was the breath of the spirit of life, all that was on the dry land, died. 23 So He destroyed all living things which were on the face of the ground: both man and cattle, creeping thing and bird of the air. They were destroyed from the earth. Only Noah and those who were with him in the ark remained alive. 24 And the waters prevailed on the earth one hundred and fifty days.

(Genesis 7:17-24)

There was no death toll; there was a living toll because it was much easier to count the eight survivors. Noah, Mrs. Noah,and their three sons with their wives, entered the ark he had worked on for 120 years and were spared only due to entering this massive floating zoo. The only animals to survive had been brought aboard also. Everything was destroyed, everything!

Part of losing hope in the storm comes with our tendency to exaggerate our loss. I've tried not to do that through this book concerning hurricane Isabel, but I probably have due to the fact I went through it. The folks from the gulf coast that survived hurricane Katrina would probably laugh at my lessons in the storm feeling I had really not even experienced a storm compared with what they had faced. As a matter of fact, if this was a book about surviving Katrina it would probably be more popular. After all, who other than folks on the east coast of North Carolina and Virginia remember Isabel.

My point is that for the people who go through the storm it makes an impact on them and on the ones close to them, but those outside their realm find it hard to see that it's that serious.

Anyone who had never been to Edenton until the past five years would say that Isabel had no effect on our town, but those who were here before the storm know the things that changed. It's the same with our personal and spiritual storms of life. People who didn't know us before the heart attack, or the break-up, or whatever the storm produced would find it hard to believe a storm had come into our life, but we know and will never be the same.

Many people choose to reject the idea that a flood came onto earth and destroyed every living thing except Noah and his family. Scientists refute it, liberal theologians explain it away, Hollywood perverts it, and it's laughed off. But for the people of Noah's day, it was real.

When these natural disasters hit there are volunteer groups ready to go and provide relief and help in recovery efforts. As a matter of fact, many of these organizations are born from a disaster in their region and now work to help others. Sometimes when I am around these people, I sense that they are hoping for a disaster so they'll have a chance to respond and have a reason to exist. Because after the storm passes and you go several years without one, people begin to wonder if we really need hurricane relief ministries and services and fewer and fewer contribute the time or finances to keep them alive.

Storms do pass over; the sun does shine again. In life even when it feels it will never end, it does and recovery and moving on seems overwhelming, but we do recover one day at a time. Time heals and moves the storm from the top of your concern list on down the line until it gets replaced by a lot of other things. You never forget it; you just don't think about it all the time.

As we have discussed throughout this book, storms have a purpose in our lives. They change us, challenge us, and make us face some things about ourselves we would never have faced on calm seas.

Peter speaks of the tendency to forget the storm in his second epistle:

> *scoffers will come in the last days, walking according to their own lusts, ⁴ and saying, "Where is the promise of His coming? For since the fathers fell asleep, all things continue as they were from the beginning of creation." ⁵ For this they willfully forget: that by the word of God the heavens were of old, and the earth standing out of water and in the water, ⁶ by which the world that then existed perished, being flooded with water.*
>
> **(II Peter 3:3-6)**

117

Part of recovering from our storms means never forgetting. Peter reminds the scoffers who reject the idea that God will judge sin that God did it before and will do it again. Next time it will not be with water but with fire. The worst thing we could do in recovering from a storm is forget and fail to learn and grow from the experience.

As Noah stepped off the ark for the first time, the sun was shining. After a long stormy spell, it just seems the sun shines brighter, and the grass is greener. I love to go outside after a storm passes. Noah is given a new day, new hope, but along with that and the lessons he has learned, a new responsibility.

Chapter 21

The New Responsibility
of Storm Survivors

Many people have the idea that to take on responsibility is something we need to avoid. Our plates are full; we have enough to worry about, and we don't need anything else to be responsible for. However Genesis 9:1 says God blessed Noah and began to give them responsibilities. To be given responsibility is a blessing. Imagine the responsibility Noah and his family faced now. Everything and every living creature have been destroyed, and now they are responsible for starting over. They must begin the task of rebuilding after the storm. They are the relief effort.

> *So God blessed Noah and his sons, and said to them:*
> *"Be fruitful and multiply, and fill the earth.*
>
> **(Genesis 9:1)**

God supplies the need; there is more than one reason He had them put these animals on the ark. Of course it was so that the animals could multiply and restore animal life to the earth. The other reason was so Noah and his family could have steak and lamb chops. Apparently up until this time, they ate only the green herbs. Now God set it up for them to eat meat as long as they cooked it well done.

> *² And the fear of you and the dread of you shall be on every beast of the earth, on every bird of the air, on all that move on the earth, and on all the fish of the sea. They are given into your hand. ³ Every moving thing that lives shall be food for you. I have given you all things, even as the green herbs. ⁴ But you shall not eat flesh with its life, that is, its blood.*
> **(Genesis 9:2-4)**

They would need this nourishment because they were to rebuild community. When God looked at all He had created in the first chapters of Genesis, He kept approving of His work by repeating the phrase **"it is good"**. But when He looked at man, Adam, and saw he was alone, He said, **"it is not good that man should be alone"**. God created man as He did many of the other creatures to live in community. Birds have flocks, cattle have herds, fish have schools, and man has community.

> *⁵ Surely for your lifeblood I will demand a reckoning; from the hand of every beast I will require it, and from the hand of man. From the hand of every man's brother I will require the life of man.*
>
> *⁶ "Whoever sheds man's blood, By man his blood shall be shed; For in the image of God He made man. ⁷ And as for you, be fruitful and multiply; Bring forth abundantly in the earth And multiply in it."*
> **(Genesis 9:5-7)**

This is why God said **"be fruitful and multiply"** He was instructing them to rebuild community and to further protect this new community rebuilding project He gave new laws concerning the value of every human life. **"*Whoever sheds man's blood, By man his blood shall be shed; For in the image of God He made man.*** Community could never be built if individuals did not value each other and respect each other.

In our efforts to restore our town in the aftermath of hurricane Isabel, it could never have been accomplished by one man, or one family, or one organization. But with the concerted efforts of community, the restoration was successful.

God has always set man up to create community. The community of Abraham's family became the focus of the Old Testament. Jesus died and rose again using twelve ragamuffin apostles filled with the Holy Spirit on the day of Pentecost to build the community of the church the Body of Christ.

These communities thrive on the basic principle God gave to Noah and his sons. Every human life is to be treated with dignity and held valuable. Communities and nations fall when human life is devalued and degraded. I must emphasize, at the risk of sounding political, it is human life not human rights that are valued in this new order after the storm. When communities and even churches begin to value politics and policies above individuals, the community suffers. When the passion for policy is greater than the passion for people, even great moves of God in communities have been brought down.

I am not saying policy is not necessary, God even sets a policy in regard to valuing human life, but the primary importance is on the human life not the policy. Jesus didn't die to end the law and policy of the Old Testament but to fulfill it that every human life might be saved from the policy's inability to save humans.

The price of taking a human life was that your own life be taken. Jesus brought out this same principle when He instructed that in His Kingdom man should "love your neighbor as yourself".

When we are in the middle of our storms there is the tendency to isolate ourselves. Survival mode often makes us self defensive and we hunker in our boats with a "every man for himself" attitude. We don't want people asking questions, we don't need people giving advice. We don't desire community we want to be left alone. It's just human nature.

To rebuild and recover from our storms, we must come out of our protective shelters and build relationships. We must begin to realize we cannot do it alone. If we fail to do this, we will never fully recover from the loss of the storm and grow from the lessons the storm was meant to teach us.

Chapter 22

The New Assurance for
Storm Survivors

Along with the great responsibility placed on Noah and his family, God entered into a new covenant relationship with them. When the responsibilities seem overwhelming and sometimes useless because of the fear that the next storm may wash away all that we do to meet the new responsibility, God gives a new promise. We are not left with the responsibility alone.

God had just finished letting them know what they were responsible for, and I think it's neat the way He begins the next part;

> *⁸ Then God spoke to Noah and to his sons with him, saying:*
> *⁹ "And as for Me, behold, I establish My covenant with you*
> *and with your descendants after you, ¹⁰ and with every living*
> *creature that is with you: the birds, the cattle, and every*
> *beast of the earth with you, of all that go out of the ark, every*
> *beast of the earth. ¹¹ Thus I establish My covenant with you:*
> **(Genesis 9:8-11)**

It's as if He's saying you have a lot to do, but I want you to know you're not in this alone, ***"as for Me"*** here's what I'm going to do. God is promising His job will be to protect them and be their security.

> ***Never again shall all flesh be cut off by the waters of the flood; never again shall there be a flood to destroy the earth."***
> **(Genesis 9:11)**

This storm had accomplished its purpose, and God assured them He would not send it again in this magnitude. He did not promise that it wouldn't rain, and that another storm would not come but that His purpose was fulfilled, and He was in control. Then He put a rainbow in the sky as a sign or token of His covenant with Noah.

> *¹² And God said: "This is the sign of the covenant which I make between Me and you, and every living creature that is with you, for perpetual generations: ¹³ I set My rainbow in the cloud, and it shall be for the sign of the covenant between Me and the earth. ¹⁴ It shall be, when I bring a cloud over the earth, that the rainbow shall be seen in the cloud; ¹⁵ and I will remember My covenant which is between Me and you and every living creature of all flesh; the waters shall never again become a flood to destroy all flesh. ¹⁶ The rainbow shall be in the cloud, and I will look on it to remember the everlasting covenant between God and every living creature of all flesh that is on the earth." ¹⁷ And God said to Noah, "This is the sign of the covenant which I have established between Me and all flesh that is on the earth."*
> **(Genesis 9:12-17)**

Scientifically the rainbow is a prism. There are only three primary colors that exist, red, blue and yellow. All the other colors such as pastels that my wife raves about are from these primary colors. What we see are the way light affects these colors in our eyes. The light rays of the sun which are not visible to us hit the moisture in the clouds which we do see and break the moisture into a prism of colors. Hence the rainbow appears, and we see it. One of the most beautiful visions on earth, if you see it in its glory, is a rainbow.

God, who we often cannot see in our storms, is light. The storm, which is often all we can see while it is raging, is darkness. The rainbow appears as the storm dissipates, and the light of God's protection and faithfulness shines into and breaks up the clouds of despair, and something beautiful appears at the end of our storm.

If it were not for the clouds, there would be no rainbow. Without the storms that come into our lives, we could never appreciate the beauty of the sun and God's light which is always there. The storms that God allows and sometimes sends into our lives have a glory of their own.

Be still, sad heart! and cease repining;
Behind the clouds is the sun still shining;

Section VI – Recovering from the Storm

In this last section of the book we looked at Noah and his family. They were the only people on earth to survive the ultimate storm and experience the sunshine again. With Noah's new day came new responsibilities and new assurances from God.

Scriptural Reading: II Corinthians 4:7-12

6 For it is the God who commanded light to shine out of darkness, who has shone in our hearts to give the light of the knowledge of the glory of God in the face of Jesus Christ.

7 But we have this treasure in earthen vessels, that the excellence of the power may be of God and not of us. 8 We are hard-pressed on every side, yet not crushed; we are perplexed, but not in despair; 9 persecuted, but not forsaken; struck down, but not destroyed- 10 always carrying about in the body the dying of the Lord Jesus, that the life of Jesus also may be manifested in our body. 11 For we who live are always delivered to death for Jesus' sake, that the life of Jesus also may be manifested in our mortal flesh. 12 So then death is working in us, but life in you.

Jesus in His Sermon on the Mount told His followers that they were "the light of the world." Paul goes in this text to speak of this light as a treasure hidden in our earthen vessels speaking of our bodies. The only way that light hidden in us can shine is through the breaking of the vessel. The storms are the things that break us and allow God's light to shine through.

1. Do you remember when you came to realize your last storm had passed?

2. Maybe your last storm made changes and things would never be the same but the anxiety and worry were gone and you slept. Did you learn anything about yourself or God that you may not have realized without the storm?

3. Is there anyone that was allowed to see the light of God's grace in you as your rode out the storm?

4. Do you now have a sense of new responsibility, a closer walk with Christ, a new purpose and assurance as a result of the storm?

Don't let the things you learned in the storm be affected by the sunshine and soft winds you're experiencing now.

Authors Comments

In 1997 Sabastian Junger released a book entitled "The Perfect Storm" based on a true story about the crew of a fishing boat the "Andrea Gail" that was hit by an unusual storm system in the Atlantic Ocean off the Northeastern US coast. The book was later remade into a movie starring George Clooney and Mark Wahlberg in 2000. I saw the movie with my wife because I knew she secretly had a crush on George Clooney from his ER television days.

The storm that hit in 1991 was unusual in that it was in fact the converging of three different storm systems. Hence it was dubbed "the perfect storm."

At the time of writing this book, my wife and I are going through what might be called a perfect storm. This storm has raged into our lives from several different areas. Our children are experiencing some storms of their own making, and we are being tossed due to our love for them. I am experiencing a career change with the ministry I have worked in for the past ten years being over. This change has created some major financial dilemmas, and the need to relocate again. The dark clouds of financial problems loom over our head, and the dreaded tossing of diabetes is creating havoc on my kidney function and has my doctor concerned.

I don't say all this to get your pity but to help you understand as you read this book that I am no stranger to storms. Mine are no worse than the storms you are going through or have experienced, but they're mine.

I remember a song my mother use to make me sing with her in church. Notice I said made me, like the disciples in the storm story from section two, I had other plans. The song was an old Dottie Rambo southern gospel song called "Thank You for the Valley." It spoke of the fact that if life were all sunshine, the flowers would die. The rivers would be deserts all barren and dry. So it thanked God for the valleys and storms of life. I'm not sure

I'm there. I'm grateful for the blessings but find it hard to be thankful for the current situation I am in.

However I do think this storm has been what has woken me up to write this book. This is my feeble attempt at "water-walking" and getting out of the boat. I am resetting my priority list, and I am so thankful that before this storm ever hit, I have learned to walk in fellowship with my Savior.

I know this storm will pass, and pray I will grow closer to Him as a result of it. May He be glorified at what He is doing to conform me to His image. I admit, however, I wish it would end soon.

My greatest desire is that it will be of some help to you as you face the storm you are in or the one that may be coming around the next bend. I'm not a weather forecaster and don't want to be a prophet of doom but remember what Longfellow said; **Thy fate is the common fate of all, Into each life some rain must fall, Some days must be dark and dreary.**

Throughout this book I have emphasized the deity of Christ in our storms. In Christ we find the power to overcome and endure the storms that come our way. However in closing I want to bring out a thought from the humanity of Christ. You see, the Jesus we serve is not only 100% God but 100% man.

The writer of the book of Hebrews brings out a fact concerning the humanity of Christ:

> *[14] Seeing then that we have a great High Priest who has passed through the heavens, Jesus the Son of God, let us hold fast our confession. [15] For we do not have a High Priest who cannot sympathize with our weaknesses, but was in all points tempted as we are, yet without sin. [16] Let us therefore come boldly to the throne of grace, that we may obtain mercy and find grace to help in time of need.*
> **(Hebrews 4:14-16)**

Isaiah in his messianic prophecy said of the Christ:

*³ He is despised and rejected by men, A Man
of sorrows and acquainted with grief.*

(Isaiah 53:3)

Jesus the master of our stormy seas as the Son of God, has experienced His own storm of life. As the Son of Man he has wept at the stormy sea of a grave, faced rejection, false accusations heartache and sorrow. Jesus understands the pain of prayers of desperation in asking God to allow the cup to pass from Him and the surrender to the storm as He accepts God's will not His own will.

Not only as God is He able to calm our seas but as man He is able to be touched by the feelings of our pain and hurt. That is why the writer of the Hebrews passages encourages us to go to Him our great high priest and find grace to help.

Even when we cannot understand what He is doing with this storm, He does understand our hurt and our pain and can give grace to help in the time of need. To be in fellowship with Him is to have access to His power to calm our storms and access to His grace to understand our pain.